4 50/7

GOETHE'S KEY TO FAUST

GOETHE'S KEY TO FAUST

A Scientific Basis for Religion and
Morality and for a Solution of the
Enigma of Evil

BY

WILLIAM PAGE ANDREWS

KENNIKAT PRESS, INC./PORT WASHINGTON, N. Y.

PT
1925
A6
1968

GOETHE'S KEY TO FAUST

Copyright 1913 by William Page Andrews
Reissued in 1968 by Kennikat Press

Library of Congress Catalog Card No: 67-27573

Manufactured in the United States of America

PREFACE

THE present résumé of a more extended epitome of all
that Goethe has said or written on the subject dealt
with in his *Faust*, is called "Goethe's Key to Faust,"
because it confines itself to that Author's own exposition
of the poem; which he said directly was intended to
enable his readers to "solve the enigmas of their own
lives," and to furnish them with a scientific basis for a
rational religious belief.

The citations are made from the cheaper edition of the
Werke, the Cotta'sche edition, or the collection of *Briefe*
by Phillip Stein, and the English translations of the
Bohn Library Edition, where it was possible to do so, for
the benefit of students to whom the more extensive
and expensive editions are not readily accessible.

The present writer proposes to set forth this Goethean
view of the subject at greater length in the form of Notes
to accompany the text of a new translation.

WILLIAM PAGE ANDREWS.

VILLA FEDERICO, CAPRI, ITALY,
June, 1912

INTRODUCTION

"Ihre Dichtung stammte von jeder aus Ihrer ganzen
Natur- und Welt-ansicht."

(HUMBOLDT TO GOETHE.)

"Faust may be regarded as a synthesis of world and
spirit, which gives us the most blessed assurance of the
eternal harmony of all Being."

(GOETHE.)

GOETHE's mastery of poetic form is so complete that
the English-speaking world is inclined to forget that he
was also, as Haeckel has said, "the greatest German
natural philosopher." Yet Humboldt most highly valued
Goethe's scientific attainments; Helmholtz said of
Goethe's ideas and discoveries in the field of natural
science that "they first raised botany and zoölogy to the
rank of actual sciences"; and Alfred Kirchoff speaks of
them as "the lightning flash, which broke up the darkness of centuries and poured a flood of light over the
world of life."

One of his latest biographers, Bielschowsky, calls attention to the fact that Goethe has also done for the
cause of religion what he has admittedly accomplished
in the realm of natural science; viz.: he has raised it
from the region of abstract speculation to the rank of
actual science, by basing his religious conclusions on the
observation of the whole great chain of natural phenomena and their interrelation; instead of on metaphysical subtilties, which a sceptical, scientific age refuses to
accept, unless they can be shown to be in accord with

what can be perceived by the senses as existing in the processes of Nature itself. The modern world is, indeed, more and more coming to believe that there *is* no adequate reason for action other than self-interest; and it has even elevated the "right to the pursuit of happiness" into a political axiom.

Goethe would show us that this idea is directly at variance with all that can be observed in Nature and Man of the laws and sequences which govern the course of existence. He would make it evident that disbelief in a Controlling Power of life, and the consequent idea of an unlimited freedom to pursue happiness as an aim in itself, is a fatally destructive mistake; from which error most of the miseries of mankind can be shown to arise.

He sets this forth at length in two passages in *Wilhelm Meister's Travels*. Speaking of religious expressions of this idea of control and of the punishment which follows violation of the moral law, Goethe there remarks: "Religious expressions become trite to us: the kernel which they should have contained has escaped us. So he would make us observe the danger of our position, how precarious must be our divergence from the tradition with which, from our youth up, so much had been associated: this is in the highest degree dangerous, particularly in the state of imperfection of our own minds. It is true that religion, practiced every day and hour, at last becomes only a pastime, and acts as a sort of police upon the outward demeanour, but no longer on the depths of the understanding: the only remedy for that is to call forth from our own hearts thoughts equally valid, equally effective, and equally soothing in a moral sense." [1]

[1] *Wilhelm Meister's Travels*, Book III, Chap. XIII, p. 400. *Wanderjähre*, p. 346.

Somewhat later in the same chapter he sets forth how this Control, which constantly subjects man to the "test" of his ability to be of service, manifests itself in man's consciousness, viz.: —

"Every human being, from the earliest moment of his life, is first unconscious, then half-conscious, and at last wholly so: he finds himself forever controlled, limited in his position; but as no one knows the end and aim of his existence, or rather, as its secret is withheld by the hand of the Most High, he therefore only gropes about, grasps at, leaves hold, stands still, moves, lingers and worries, and so on in manifold ways, as all the errors which confuse us arise.

"Even the wisest is compelled in daily life to be wise for the moment, and by that means attains no enlightenment in the universal. Seldom does he know for certain whither he has to turn in the future, and what he really has to do and to leave undone.

"Happily all these, and yet a hundred other wondrous questions, are answered by your incessantly active course of life. Persevere in direct observance of the day's duty; and thereby *test* the purity of your heart, and the safety of your soul. If thus in unoccupied hours you aspire, and find opportunity to elevate yourself, you will so gain a right attitude towards the Sublime, to which we must in every way reverently surrender ourselves; regard every occurrence with veneration, and acknowledge therein a higher guidance." [1]

We see from the extracts, above quoted, that Goethe's intention is to give us a new basis for religious belief, by setting forth that right attitude towards the Primal Source of Life, which he would impress upon his

[1] *Wilhelm Meister's Travels*, pp. 402–03. *Wanderjähre*, p. 348.

readers, and, by showing the action of the controlling, creative Power of Life, the sequences of the effects thereof in this mirror of Life itself.

This "greatest natural philosopher" does not philosophize; but, as one of the characters herein says, he has in this drama of life "lent us his own eyes" to see for ourselves the operation of the laws of all existence. He does not dogmatize, but selects and arranges the facts of life so vividly before us that the philosophic conclusions are inevitable, and we must make them for ourselves from the evidence thus laid before us.

This is the *Faust* of Goethe. As Humboldt suggests, it is the result of, and epitomizes, all his observation of Nature and of the world.[1]

Goethe through the mouth of Mephistopheles[2] indicates one reason for his embodying his philosophy of life in a poetical trope, a figure of speech, rather than stating his ideas directly. Mephistopheles there remarks: that man is not pleased with pure truth when it is given to him didactically; but, if it is suggested in a manner which forces him to think it out for himself, he then finally imagines it is his own, and prizes it as of great value.

There are also other advantages of the method adopted, as Goethe intimates in an epigrammatic distich, which gives us another idea of his reason for pursuing this course: —

"Lyres Apollo bestirs, but he draweth the death-dealing bow too:
  While he the shepherds may charm, he stretches th' Python in
    sand." [3]

---

[1] *Humboldt to Goethe*, January 6, 1832. *Graef*, p. 599.
[2] *Faust*, II, Act II, Sc. I, line 6744.
[3] *Gedichte*, "*In Antiker Form*," *Werke*, I, p. 160.

That is, it enables the author to express his full and true opinion on all subjects, political, theological, scholastic, or other matter with entire freedom, to attack all such unreal speculations as may seem to him a hindrance, rather than a help to a faith in a Controlling Power; and to indulge in what sarcasm he will without fear of consequences to himself, or of injury to readers not in a condition of mind to receive his message in full; for, as his hero says to his heroine, "he would rob no one of his faith, nor of his church"; and he is therefore careful to conceal his whole opinion on many subjects from persons who would misunderstand them to their own detriment.

In the First Part of this drama of life, which part he tells us is "entirely subjective," he gives us an exact and vivid image of his own futile strivings to solve the problem of life by means of metaphysical erudition, and of the effect thereof upon his own life, as resulting in a suicidal mania consequent upon his loss of faith in any Controlling Power. He then shows us the further effect, in his own individual case, of the false notion arising from this loss of faith, that life may be devoted to "the pursuit of happiness" as an aim in itself. This is represented as a delusion of the Destructive, from whence all the miseries thereafter following are seen to spring. In showing also the beneficial results of these ills on the individual and on the whole progression of life, he suggests a solution of that troublesome enigma of evil, which is the great hindrance to a rational faith. He then exhibits the one and only way of happiness, as being the way of *service*, the functioning of the individual part in accord with the evolutionary tendency of all existence.

In the Second Part he suggests, as he says, "the whole

history of the world, in all its varied phases of activity, for three thousand years" ; as illustrating, in the occurrence of like sequences,. the universal tendency of all existence, of which the previous life of the individual was the mirror in miniature.

The aim of the present volume is not, however, to discuss the subject from the outside; but closely to follow the method of elucidation recommended by the poet himself; that is, to collate what he has said of the theme, with only such additions as may be necessary to show the relation between the poet's life and thought and its expression in the poem itself, and the connection of "every smallest part with this underlying idea of the whole."

The test of the value of any elucidation consists in its adequately setting forth this relation, both to the subject as a whole, and to the incidents of Goethe's own life; and this intention is the motive of the present undertaking.

GOETHE'S KEY TO FAUST

SCHOLAR

"If one an indication only had,
'T would let one further feel the way."
                    (*Faust*, i, lines 2007–08.)

MEPHISTOPHELES

"Here, take this key.

FAUST

"It is a little thing.

MEPHISTOPHELES

"First grasp it, and not lightly valuing.
This key will scent it out, the place that's right,
Follow it down; it leads you to — THE MOTHERS.

"Then on! these magic methods re-arrange
The incense mists, that into Gods will change."
                    (*Faust*, ii, lines 6259–6302.)

"The Nature Genius by the hand
Should lead thee on through all the land,
The whole of life should show to thee,
The wond'rous weavings of humanity;
All may for thee therein occur,
As in a magic casket 't were."
(*Hans Sachsens Poetische Sendung, Werke*, II, p. 18.)

"If this casket betokens anything, then in time the key must be found for it . . . I cannot refrain from recognising in this the destinies of the Christian Religion, which, often divided and scattered, must yet meet at last at the Cross" (i.e., in *Renunciation*).
(*Wilhelm Meister's Travels*, Book I, Chap. XII, pp. 145–46. *Wanderjähre*, p. 131.)

"The little key of your ornamental casket has been found."
(*Wilhelm Meister's Travels*, Book III, Chap. II, p. 294. *Wanderjähre*, p. 258.)

"Some hint may be given of this marvellous finding, refinding, separating, and reuniting."
(*Wilhelm Meister's Travels*, Book III, Chap. VII, p. 352. *Wanderjähre*, p. 307.)

"He pulled out the broken key entire . . . the two ends adhered to each other by magnetic *Attraction*."
(*Wilhelm Meister's Travels*, Book III, Chap. XVIII, p. 435. *Wanderjähre*, p. 374.)

GOETHE'S KEY TO FAUST

> "In the observation of a work of art we must always
> have in mind the lofty, unattainable idea. . . . We
> must seek to penetrate to the ultimate source of the
> artist's theory and practice."
>
> (*Der Sammler und die Seinigen, Werke,* xxx, *Briefe,*
> iv, p. 49.)

> "Though you may also have deeply hidden away the
> noble treasures, they are ready to be discovered by the
> human intellect. Nature in her wide realm is always
> suitable, consistent, and unvarying; and whoever holds
> the tender end of the clue may indeed follow on through
> the twisted labyrinth of the world."
>
> (*Festgedichte,* January 30, 1828. *Werke,* ii, p. 178.)

GOETHE'S COMMENTS ON HIS COMMENTATORS

BECAUSE Goethe, referring to his method of production, said he did not start from an abstract idea and
strive to embody this idea in the incidents of the drama,
some commentators of his *Faust* have declared that no
such central idea is to be found therein; notwithstand-
ing the fact that Goethe himself has repeatedly said that
there was such "thought and idea of the whole," which
the intelligent reader must grasp and bring to the elucidation of each part.[1] He also said he had found such a
central idea in life itself, of which the scenes of the
drama are the vivid images; and further, that he had
"taken great pains to adapt even the smallest portion
thereunto."

[1] *Pniower,* No. 853, p. 257.

He said that the difficulty in understanding a poem like *Faust* arose, because: "Few Germans, and perhaps few persons of any modern nation can appreciate an æsthetic whole." "The mistake," he says, "that the commentators had made was to attempt to explain isolated passages by themselves, and not in their relation to this idea of the whole: or they do not believe in simplicity and so involve the subject in a mass of metaphysical speculations about it, which confuse instead of illuminating the reader." He says, "it annoys men to find that truth is so simple"; [1] and he tells us that "the true, good, and excellent are always simple"; it is error which is ever highly manifold and contradictory. [2] Goethe was constantly setting forth that the world of life is "so simple"; and he wrote to Zelter (March 29, 1827), that "one must believe in simplicity if one would go the right way"; he also wrote Zelter that the difficulty in understanding this drama had arisen because "people seek entrance to a poem everywhere except through the door"; . . . "or are incapable of recognising æsthetic or higher moral aims." [3]

This "door," through which we must enter, the poet has furnished in the two "Prologues" prefixed to the First Part of the drama; which Prologues set forth the intention, the poet's method, and that "lofty idea" to which we "must seek to penetrate." He has also told us directly that the incidents of the First Part "were all drawn from his own inner and outer experiences"; which we must know if we would understand this image of them.

Speaking of J. J. Ampère's point of view of his work,

[1] *Sprueche, Werke*, IV, p. 224.   [2] *Sprueche, Werke*, IV, p. 177.
[3] *Goethe to Zelter*, April 14, 1816, p. 129.

Goethe said: "When critics start from philosophy, and in the consideration and discussion of a poetical production proceed in a manner which they intend as an elucidation, it is often only intelligible to philosophers of their own school; while for other people it is far more obscure than the work upon which they intended to throw a light. M. Ampère, on the contrary, shows himself quite practical and popular. He exhibits the relation between the production and the producer, and judges the different poetical productions as different fruits of the different epochs of the poet's life. He has studied most profoundly the changing course of my earthly career and of the condition of my mind; and has had the faculty of seeing what I have not expressed, and what, so to speak, could only be read between the lines. . . . Then, concerning Faust, his remarks are no less clever, since he not only notes as parts of himself the gloomy, discontented striving of the principal character, but also the scorn and bitter irony of Mephistopheles." [1]

For the enlightenment of his countrymen, Goethe translated from the French, and published in German, these remarks of Ampère, about his work, referred to in the previous paragraph. They are as follows: —

"This is his *Faust*, that curious profound creation, that wonderful drama in which every grade of being is made to appear before us; from the God of Heaven to the spirits of darkness, from humanity to the beast, and deeper still to those misformed creatures, which, like Shakespeare's Caliban, could only owe their awful existence to the poet's power of imagination. One finds in this singular work the whole series of perfect models of every kind of writing, from the rudest buffoonery to the

[1] *Eckermann*, May 3, 1827, p. 251.

most exalted lyric poetry; one finds every sort of human feeling and sentiment here depicted, from the most repulsive to the tenderest, from the blackest darkness to those which are the sweetest of all.

"While I must continue to confine myself to the historical standpoint, and may only undertake to seek the personality of the poet in his works, I may congratulate myself that we can see in *Faust* the fullest expression thereof which the poet has given of himself. This *Faust* indeed, that he seized upon in his youth and completed in his ripest old age, this conception that he bore with him through all the agitations of his life, as Camoëns carried his poem with him through the waves, this *Faust* possessed him wholly. Was not the young poet himself distressed by the passion for knowledge, and the martyrdom of doubt? Whence came the thought to him, to flee into a supernatural realm, to call to him the invisible powers? Was he not himself plunged for a long time in the visions of the *illuminati;* which even gave him the idea *that he would be able to invent a religion?* This irony of Mephistopheles, who sports so wantonly with the weakness and desires of mankind, is not all this the disdainful, mocking side of the poet's spirit? Has it not a relation to that vexation of spirit, of which some trace betrays itself in the earliest years of his life; a bitter leaven thrown into a strong soul through a precocious satiety?

"Especially in the character of Faust, the man whose burning, unwearied heart can neither do without happiness, nor enjoy it; who gives himself unconditionally away, and yet regards himself with distrust; who is fettered alike by the enthusiasm of passion, and the despondency of despair; is not this a persuasive revelation of the most secret and the most agitated part of the soul of the poet?

"And now to complete the picture of his inner life, he has represented, in that most lovely figure of Margaret, an exalted memorial of a young maiden, with whom he believed himself to be in love when he was but fourteen years old; whose image ever hovered around him, and imparted some lineaments of her character to all his heroines. This heavenly self-surrender of a naïve, pious, and tender heart is wonderfully contrasted with the sensual and dark out-reaching of the lover; who follows, in the midst of his dream of love, the phantom of his imaginative power and the satiety of his thoughts; over-whelmed with the sorrows of the soul, but not extin-guished; and who is distressed with unconquerable need of joy and the bitter feeling that, hard as it may be, one must experience and impart it."[1]

In writing of a French translation of his *Faust* by M. Stapfer, Goethe said: "*Faust* forever embodies and firmly retains the period of development of the human spirit, that was pained and also tormented by all that tortures and torments humanity, by all that disquiets mankind, and has too laid hold on them; and we are to see that mankind, like his Faust, has been blessed, as well by that which men abominate, as by that in favor of which they are prepossessed, and which they have desired."[2]

We must, however, not lose sight of the fact that these illuminating observations on the subject of *Faust* refer

[1] *Auswaertige Litteratur. Franzoesische Litteratur*, II. *Werke*, XXVIII, pp. 51–52. *Pniower*, No. 464, p. 157.

[2] *Auswaertige Litteratur. Franzoesische Litteratur*, II. *Werke*, XXVIII, p. 77.

only to that First Part of the poem which was produced,
he tells us, at a period when the poet himself was in a
state of "semi-darkness" as to the meaning of life.

If we would "further know what he knows" and what
he has embodied in his *Faust*, we must, as he said, "look
into his life and works." He has also told us that he
scattered the *keys* to its elucidation all through the text
of the poem itself; and in many speeches of the characters introduced, the poet speaks directly to the reader
with the intention of elucidating the context.

To find his *Faust* that "easy matter to understand,"
which the poet predicts it would be found to be if we follow his advice, we must first fully grasp the "lofty idea,"
which he tells us we must always "keep in mind," and
the relation thereto of all the varying portions of the
poem.

We must now examine what Goethe himself has
said : —

First : of the existence of such an idea, and where we
may find the statement thereof.

Second : what that intention is *not*, and then what it
is.

Third : what method he has pursued in carrying out
his intention, and incorporating in the text
itself both the idea and its elucidation.

We shall thus arrive at a comprehension of the whole
poem, which will prove to be a sufficient "Key" to
unlock all its enigmas.

OF THE EXISTENCE OF AN INTENTION

Goethe wrote to Knebel (November 14, 1827): "The chief intention (*Hauptintention*) is clear and the whole significant [i.e. of the underlying theme]. The individual parts will also become so [i.e. clear and significant] if one does not observe and undertake to explain them separately; but they will elucidate themselves if regarded in their relation to the whole" [the theme of the drama].[1]

He says elsewhere that the difficulty has been that people have not first sought this underlying theme; and he wrote to Zelter: "If people would only look for the physical — moral — æsthetic problems, which I have scattered so plentifully throughout my work and apply them to themselves, they would thus solve the enigmas of their own lives." [2]

WHAT WAS NOT THE POET'S INTENTION

We have first to note that this intention was NOT the presentation of a drama for theatrical representation; therefore, all criticism based on the theatrical point of view is inapplicable to the subject.

Goethe wrote to Foster that "*Faust* was not written or thought of from the beginning as a play for stage representation." [3]

---

[1] *Graef*, p. 421. *Pniower*, No. 585.
[2] *Goethe to Zelter*, December 4, 1827, p. 310.
[3] *Graef*, p. 442.

THE UNDERLYING IDEA

"The true power of a poem consists in the *motif*."
(*Goethe to Eckermann*, Jan. 18, 1825, p. 107.)

THIS "motif" is the idea underlying all the varied scenes and episodes of the drama. Goethe has directly told us what this is, viz: "The *Causa Finalis* of the world and human affairs is the true *motif* of poetic dramatic art." [1]

"One thinks of the greatness of the ancients as setting forth before the eyes the Source, and the rule of conduct of all life and activity, not as an empty speculation, but as an incentive to life and deed." [2]

As early as 1770 he wrote to Herder of his then vague intentions concerning the idea of his Faust: "I now study the life and death of the hero and make the dialogue in my mind. It is as yet only a dim presentiment, . . . " He goes on to suggest that "the subject is the power of evil, . . . or rather the divine call to the teacher of mankind . . ." He says he "needs time to develop the subject," and doubts whether he will do it as a fable, like Æsop, or La Fontaine, or like Plato as a gilded idol, . . . or whether he "*can rise to the height of a true religion*." [3]

It is not the poet's intention to discredit religion, but rather to furnish an incorruptible basis for a real reli-

[1] *Goethe to Charlotte von Stein*, March 3, 1785, *Stein*, III, p. 44.
[2] *Sprueche in Prosa, Maximen und Reflexionen*, VI, *Werke*, IV, p. 161.
[3] *Goethe to J. G. Herder*, end of 1771, undated, *Stein*, I, p. 161.

gion, and to show that any religion is true *in so far* as its
tenets conform to what can be observed of the action of
this *Causa Finalis*, which mankind under many names
calls his God.

This is set forth in the First Prologue, where "The
Poet"[1] says it is the poet's business to assure us of the
existence of this *Causa Finalis* ("*sichert den Olymp*");
and to show the essential unity in all the varied forms of
religion that have striven to set forth the idea of such an
Ultimate Cause; which unity he there expresses as a uniting of the Gods ("*vereinet Goetter*"). This is that "conception of Faust" of which Goethe wrote to Humboldt
(March 17, 1832) as existing "for over sixty years."[2]

Goethe says that the subject of where and how this
Primal Cause of all activity manifests itself in the results of its action was not in youth clear to him. He was
at first "as one that walks in the twilight"; but as the
subject opened out to his view " from the different gradients of life's pyramid," he wrote this or that other
scene of this drama of life, to embody his realization of
the presence and action of this Power in the special
manifestation of life before him.

On April 14, 1798, he wrote to Frau v. Schiller that he
was then revising what was already written, so that "the
smallest portion will be adapted to the whole mass: the
harmony with what follows is most significantly in-
creased." [3]

Goethe directly states the fact that there *is* in the
poem such a central idea; which thought is the revelation, in all events, of the action of the beneficent control
exercised by the Creative Power. He also reiterates this
in the last speech of the completed drama; which speech

[1] *Faust,* i, line 156.   [2] *Graef,* p. 606.   [3] *Graef,* p. 75.

assures us that all of the past is only a symbol of the
controlling action of a Power unreachable with our
imagination, which is seen operative in the events of
life; an indescribable power, visible as an Eternal-
feminine influence, which evolves life and leads man
upward and onward. This is that theme with which the
poem opens and also closes, and Goethe has told us that
it is a theme to which all the incidents of the drama are
adapted as illustrations thereof.

Goethe sees this *Causa Finalis* of life as a creative
force controlling all life; a force constantly giving itself
forth in creative action, evolving itself and sustaining
the life produced. He has elsewhere remarked that "the
highest visible manifestation of this Creative Source of
life which we poor mortals are capable of perceiving" is
to be seen in the creative, life-sustaining action of the
Sun; to which action all earthly existence owes its being.

We must here pause to note well that the Sun (*Die
Sonne*, in German) is feminine, not masculine; a distinc-
tion most important in the development of the Goethean
theory of existence; but which has been overlooked by
his commentators, and also by translators who have not
adhered to the exact phraseology of the original text.

Goethe first calls our attention to the fact that the
whole solar system is controlled by this central source of
life, the Sun; which control is exercised by a power of
attraction that holds "*her* brother-spheres," the planets,
on their prescribed course. Modern Science also observes that meteoric bodies, which leave this circling
progression, fall back into the Sun, and are given out
again as life-creating warmth; as the materials of which
human bodies are composed are dissolved and recom-
posed after death into new forms of life.

Goethe sees a similar manifestation of this Creative Power in the irresistible power of attraction exercised by the life-creating, life-sustaining force of the passion of love. This power of attraction manifests itself in the attractive force of Beauty in Woman, which controls the course of life of the men about her (as the Sun controls the course of the planets), and this Power leads men on to creative action in accord with itself.

Because Woman's action in exercising this power of attraction and in giving forth herself, not only to reproduce life, but also to sustain the life so created and to evolve and bring it on to higher development, is so exactly similar in character to what we can observe of that manifestation of the Creative Source of life visible in the activities of the Sun; therefore this *Causa Finalis* of all existence is characterized by Goethe as *"Das Ewig-weibliche."* To visualize this idea he, at the end of the drama, utilizes the Church's figure of the Mother of God, *"The Mater Gloriosa, soaring in the Heavens,"* as the image of what we can observe in the Universe above, and in the life about us, of the operation of that Creative Power of which men have no clear conception based on observation; but which they have been taught to adore as "God, The Creator."

The guiding, controlling power of feminine attraction, "in its relation to our solar system," "as something one may hardly venture to express," is suggested by Goethe in a chapter of his *Wilhelm Meister* devoted to this subject.[1]

If we observe that the happiness which follows the creative action of love is the result of our individual activ-

---

[1] *Wilhelm Meister's Travels,* Book III, Chap. xv, pp. 426–27. *Wanderjähre,* p. 367.

ity being thus in harmony with the creative, controlling
tendency of the whole of existence; and that the like
result, from the same accord, follows in every depart-
ment of human activity, then we have learned something of the laws governing all existence, and have thus
mastered the secret of happiness; which, Goethe tells
us, it is the poet's intention to impart, by showing us all
the various activities of mankind, and their relations to
the controlling tendency of life.[1]

Schiller observed this central idea of the poem, and,
writing to Goethe of what he found therein, said: "You
look at Nature as a whole: when seeking to get light
thrown upon her individual parts, you look for the explanation of the individual in the totality of all her various manifestations." [2]

Goethe himself said of a work of art in general: "The
horizon of the active power of the creative genius must
be as widely extended as Nature herself: that is to say,
the organization [of the work of art] must be so finely
interwoven and offer such an endless number of points
of contact with the stream of Nature which surrounds
all things, that all the relations of [the phenomena of]
Nature, as they exist in the great [world about us] must
here in the small [space of the representation] seem to
stand near to each other and yet have room to act. . . .
All these relations of this great whole of which the creative genius has merely a dim presentiment, must necessarily in some wise become either visible, audible, or
comprehensible through the power of the imagination
. . . all these revelations must be seized and illuminated

---

[1] *See Wilhelm Meister's Apprenticeship*, Book II, Chap. II, p. 69.
Lehrjähre, p. 81.
[2] *Schiller to Goethe*, August 23, 1794.

as by a burning point, where converging rays of light are assembled; that the connection between them may appear as completely, in the little circumference of the representation, as they do in the great whole of Nature itself." [1]

In resuming work on his *Faust*, Goethe wrote to Schiller, that "their Hans Sachs studies" had "led him back on this dusky cloudy way." That *way* is the early, dim presentiment that the Cause is revealed in the results of the operations of existence, both when these activities are directly creative and when they seem merely destructive. The early portions of the drama owe much in form to the poetry of Hans Sachs, and in his poem entitled *Hans Sachs' Poetische Sendung*, Goethe sets forth what his own mission in *Faust* has been, viz.: "I have selected much for you in the confusing tumult of existences in the world, that you may have clear thought and begin nothing ineptly": [that is, with an imperfect realization of the ultimate result of the action of these confused existences.] "And so the world shall stand before you, its enduring life and virility; its inner proportions and fixed laws. The Nature Genius shall lead you by the hand through all countries and shall show you the whole of life; marvellous activities of humanity, its confusions, seekings, strivings, and impulses. . . . And you may see all these happenings as if they occurred before you in a *magic casket*." [2] Note again the figure of "*the casket*."

In speaking of the scientific observation of life, Goethe refers to it as a developing revelation, "a synthesis of

[1] *Ueber die bildende Nachahmung des Schoenen, Werke*, XXIII. *Italien*, p. 168.

[2] *Werke*, II, p. 18.

world and spirit" (*Geist*); which synthesis "gives us the blessed assurance of the eternal harmony of all Being." [1] He remarks elsewhere that "Men say the phenomenon is a consequence without basis, an effect without cause. It is so difficult for mankind to find basis and primal cause, because they are so simple they have hidden themselves from sight."

Goethe wrote from Rome that he "has found a principle that carries him through the labyrinth of human development like the thread of Ariadne." [2] This principle is the idea of the Control exercised by the progressive movement of the whole, the constant evolution of life, which controls life, as the movement of a stream controls all things that move within its current.

Goethe directly compares the progressive movement of all life to that of a stream: "Life is a stream, we must not obstruct or act against it"; [3] i.e., our action must be in accord with and serviceable to the movement; or we shall be only a hindrance thereto and be overwhelmed thereby.

The suggestion in Goethe's *Wilhelm Meister*, that the poet's mission is to point out to man the one and only way to happiness, has been alluded to; and, in this drama, Goethe would show us that this *way* consists in renunciation of all else, to the one aim of bringing our personal action into accord with this universal trend of existence; the giving forth of self to forward the general progression of the whole; the functioning of the part in every direction in accord with the general progression. He says that this giving forth of self is the only abiding

---

[1] *Sprueche in Prosa, Ueber Naturwissenschaft, Werke*, IV, p. 215.
[2] *Goethe to Charlotte von Stein*, August 25, 1787, *Stein*, III, p. 173.
[3] *Riemer*, June 1807, No. 307. *Biedermann*, II, p. 171.

enjoyment. In his poem *Eins und Alles — One and All*, a section of the group of poems entitled *Gott und Welt*, where it is set forth that "The Eternal stirs in everything," Goethe clearly sets this forth: —

> "Statt heissen Wuenschen, wilden Wollen
> Statt laest'gem Fordern, strengem Sollen,
> Sich aufzugeben, ist Genuss." [1]

And this is the result which his hero Faust arrives at as the outcome of all his varied experiences. It is the universal law of life, the giving forth of self in creative action; which we are first asked to observe as characteristic of "that highest manifestation of The Creative, the Sun." "It points to that high meaning of Renunciation, by which alone" (as is also observed in *Wilhelm Meister*) "the first real entrance into life is conceivable."

But we are to note well that Goethe does not mean that this self-renunciation, which alone gives happiness, shall be carried on to the injury of the personality of the individual: that is a thing which he expressly declared is "entirely unpracticable." "It is," he says, "in opposition to all nature, all experience, and all the course of events for thousands of years; . . . each ought to begin with himself, to sharpen and improve his own faculties, to raise the standard of his own personality, and if each one does his duty as an individual, and works rightly in his own vocation, it will be well with the whole." [2]

But life, if we look only at the individual parts thereof, appears to be full of unhappiness, evils, and destructiveness. This, the so-called enigma of evil, is a problem that Goethe also proposes to solve for us, by calling our

[1] *Gedichte, "Gott und Welt," "Eins und Alles," Werke,* II, p. 127.
[2] *Eckermann,* October 20, 1830, p. 496.

attention to the result of these apparent evils on the whole controlling stream of life; from whose onward movement they also are shown to proceed, as a necessary adjunct of that beneficent progression, "the evolution of all life into something higher and better."

As he has pointed out, that happiness is the result of activity which is of service to and therefore in accord with this controlling creative tendency; so also he would make evident that unhappiness, the miseries and destruction from which men suffer, are the result of disaccord with this beneficent movement to which all life owes its existence.

If this movement should be hindered and arrested by the continuance in its progressive current of individual lives *unfit* for and unserviceable, or inimical thereunto, the benefit to the whole body of existence would be interrupted, and life itself would cease to be. In this view the miseries — which warn us that our lives are not serviceable to this control, and are not in harmony therewith — are not an evil, but a benefit to the individual, as well as to the whole movement itself; because they bring us back into harmony with the law of life, which accord is the source of happiness. The temptations which are herein shown as a necessity to stir man up to such active accord are also, in this view, not an evil; because they *test* man to prove his fitness for such service; and all action must be, as Goethe points out, of service, either directly creatively, or as aiding this creative control by removing hindrances thereunto.

This is the idea of the control exercised by this *Causa Finalis* of life; whose action Goethe has embodied in this drama of all existence, and of which he remarked: "Some men convince themselves of the Eternal, of the

Necessary, and of Immutable Law, and seek to form for themselves ideas which are incorruptible; nay, which observation of the Perishable does not shake, but rather confirms." [1]

"Nature," he says, "in no wise favors our weaknesses; but either makes something out of us, or will have nothing at all to do with us." [2] That is, she discards all that is *unfit* for the beneficial progress of the whole.

"When Nature abhors she speaks it aloud; the creature that shall not be is not produced; the creature that lives with a false life is soon destroyed. Unfruitfulness, painful existence, early destruction, these are her curses, the marks of her displeasure. . . . It is only by immediate consequences that Nature punishes. Look around you; and what is prohibited, what is accursed, will force itself upon your notice. In the silence of the convent, in the tumult of the world, a thousand practices are revered, while her curse rests upon them. On stagnant idleness, as on over-strained toil; on caprice and superfluity, as on constraint and want, Nature looks down with mournful eyes; her call is to moderation; true are all her conditions and tranquil all her operations." [3]

This Goethean view of the operation of the destructive is that which modern Science has also announced as the law of the removal of the *unfit:* it is the view suggested in *Wilhelm Meister:* Man, like the pupils there spoken of, "if he cannot suit himself to the

---

[1] *Autobiog.*, II, p. 64, *Dichtung und Wahrheit*, Teil IV, Buch XVI, *Werke*, XXI, p. 202.

[2] *Eckermann*, February 26, 1831, p. 522.

[3] *Wilhelm Meister's Apprenticeship*, Book VIII, Chap. IX, pp. 545–46. *Lehrjähre*, Teil II, p. 277.

regulations, must leave the district where they are in force." [1]

By pointing this out in the events of his drama, Goethe will strive to give us a reason for individual action, which must be in harmony with the whole movement of life. The harmony of the individual part with the trend of the whole is, in his view, also the basis of all morality; morality being the action which is in accord with the immutable law, or trend of existence.

Speaking of the use of this exposition of life in dramatic art, he said: "The worth of the morally good and beautiful could be attained by experience and wisdom; inasmuch as the bad showed itself in its consequence as a destroyer of happiness, both in the individual and the whole body; while the noble and the right seemed to produce and secure the happiness of one and all. Thus the morally beautiful could become a doctrine, and diffuse itself over whole nations as something plainly expressed. A great dramatic poet . . . may [thus] succeed in making the soul of his dramas become the soul of the people." [2]

"When the lofty idea embodies itself in a common, customary, comprehensible figure so that it meets us as if alive, present, actual; so that we can seize it, appropriate it, retain it, live with it as our equal. . . . Here a living doctrine is pronounced, a doctrine which can cause no argument: it is not an opinion about what is right and wrong; it is right and wrong themselves." [3]

Goethe wrote to a friend who had noticed and

[1] *Wilhelm Meister's Travels*, Book II, Chap. II, p. 165. *Wanderjähre*, p. 148.

[2] *Eckermann*, April 1, 1827, pp. 234-35.

[3] *Wilhelm Meister's Travels*, Book II, Chap. II, pp. 161-62. *Wanderjähre*, p. 145.

pointed out this moral intention in the drama of *Faust:*
"You are to be especially praised that you have set forth
in such a good light the poet's moral tendency and
method of procedure. The public will never learn to
comprehend that the genuine poet treats of destructiveness of the deed, the danger of the intention . . . to exhibit these in their consequences, not as a cowled peni-
tence teacher." [1]

This, the fundamental idea of this drama of life, is the
clue that leads us through its labyrinthine incidents,
and the thread which binds them all together in one
consistent whole.

"The poet," said Eckermann to Goethe, "has only to
express a manifold world. He uses the fable of the
famous hero only as a sort of thread running through
all, whereon he can string what he pleases." Goethe
then replied that he "was entirely right in this." [2]

The Boy-Charioteer in the Carnival Scene of the
Second Part — who, as Goethe has told us, is the poet
himself — suggests that it is not the conventional "Her-
ald's task to sound the depths of the goblet of life": [3]
that is the poet's mission. We are asked to note that the
gifts, which this poet has strewn among the multitude,
were strung on a thread like a necklace: but that, separated from the connection, "they buzz meaninglessly
about the ears, or seem like fragile glittering butter-
flies." [4] This, indeed, is the effect made on the general
reader by the brilliant poetical passages of this poem, if
these passages are considered separately, by them-

[1] *Goethe to J. S. Zauper,* September 7, 1821, *Stein, Goethes Briefe,*
VII, p. 283.

[2] *Graef,* p. 565. *Eckermann,* February 13, 1831, p. 507.

[3] *Faust,* II, Act I, lines 5606–08.

[4] *Faust,* II, Act I, lines 5630–39.

selves, and not in relation to the connecting idea, which binds them all together as a revelation of the action of the whole of life.

We must now regard the method in which he composed this drama, whose incidents, if we lose sight of this thread, seem so disconnected; and we must not lose sight of this fact: the poet has told us that all these incidents, even to the smallest detail, have been included because they illustrate the operation of this universal law of life.

HOW THE POET'S MOTIF IS
DEVELOPED

"There is a poetry without tropes, which is all one
trope."
(Sprueche in Prosa, Werke, IV, p. 134.)

"It is true that these threads are somewhat slack and
delicate, though they certainly run through the entire
piece, connecting what would otherwise be wholly dis-
united, and which in truth does actually become so,
when you have severed them, and fancy that you have
achieved something by leaving the ends remaining."
(Wilhelm Meister's Apprenticeship, Book v, Chap. IV,
p. 274. Lehrjähre, Teil II, p. 18.)

WE have seen that Goethe "adapted even the smallest part of the poem" to the development of the central
idea, the *motif* of the whole; and that *Faust* is all a trope,
a thing other than it seems; viz.: it is *not* the story of a
semi-historical personage, but rather an image of all life
and its relations. Goethe, in a memorandum on his
Faust, says: "The poet translates life into a picture, an
image. (*Bild*.)" [1]

He elsewhere remarked: "The true poetic genius will
set the moods of the inner life before us, as the universal,
the world-life; for the life of the individual is forever the
mirror of the life of man. . . . That is the genuine
poetry, where the individual represents the universal;
not as a dream or shadow, but as a living and visible
revelation of the Inscrutable. . . . So by means of simi-
larities and images we are carried on through the inci-

[1] *Graef*, p. 176.

dents of life to the significance of all being: and the great
mystery [of life] is by word and image, laid open before
the eyes."

Again he calls on men to "observe the whole, and
therein to learn and understand their own course of life,
and to realize the significance of the actions of many
years, as they occurred also in the life of another [i.e.,
Goethe]. The thoughts, the designs, the results of the
conditions, their relations, how one accentuates the
other." "That," he says, "will be enough." Enough,
that is, to understand "the artistic power of the artist:
how all is "well-contrived, artfully reflected on, beauti-
fully wrought and smoothly completed. As Nature
reveals in the many forms and conditions only one controlling Deity: so in the sphere of Art, there is woven a
sense of the Eternal Method."[1]

In the opening poem of Goethe's *West-oestlicher-Diwan*,
he describes the motif and method both of that poem
and of his *Faust*. He says that "amid loving and drink-
ing and singing, he will rejuvenate the source of religious
feeling. There, in the pure and the right, he will give the
human races a new impulse into the deeps of that primal
Source of Life, from which they still receive the doctrine
of Heaven in the speech of earth, and do not break their
heads to pieces over it." He says that "the Poet's words
are lightly knocking at the portals of Paradise."[2]

"Word and image are correlated; they seem ever to
seek of themselves to suggest to us their meaning in
tropes and symbols; so all which is said or sung to the

[1] *Wilhelm Meister's Travels*, Book II, Chap. IX, p. 256. *Wanderjähre*, p. 228.
[2] *West-oestlicher Diwan, Moganni Nameh, Buch des Saengers, Hegire* I,
Werke, III, p. 15.

ear, should at the same time come forth to meet the eye. So we see in early times, in Bible and fable, how word and image are ever balancing with each other." [1]

Goethe gives as the reason of his embodying his philosophy in images: "I have not become didactic in my work, a poetic representation of the conditions, in part actual, in part ideal, appears to me always the best way of setting it forth: whereby the thoughtful reader, with growing experience, may in the images find out for himself the mainfold results" [that lead to one conclusion].[2]

"It is not fit to tell others anything beyond what they can take up. A man understands nothing but what is commensurate with him. You communicate the high doctrine to your children, in the first place as a sensible sign, then with some symbolic accompaniment attached to it, and at last unfold to them its deepest meaning." [3]

Goethe speaks in his *Autobiography* of the necessity he was under in his youth to search into his own inner nature to obtain the true basis of feeling or reflection: " and thus began that tendency from which I could not deviate my whole life through; namely, the tendency to turn into an image, into a poem, everything that delighted or troubled me: all that has thus been confessed by me consists of fragments of one great confession." [4]

We must, however, carefully observe that his method is not to start from one abstract idea, and then embody

---

[1] *Sprueche in Prosa, Maximen und Reflexionen,* III, *Werke,* IV, p. 131.

[2] *Goethe to Nikolai Borehardt,* May 1, 1828, *Stein, Goethes Briefe,* VIII, p. 213.

[3] *Wilhelm Meister's Travels,* Book II, Chap. I, p. 157. *Wanderjähre,* p. 141.

[4] *Dichtung und Wahrheit,* Teil II, Buch VII, p. 257. *Autobiog.* I, Book VII, p. 240.

it in images which would form an allegory of that idea.
He said of his *Faust:* "It was not in my line, as a poet, to
strive to embody anything *abstract.* I received into my
mind impressions, and those of a sensual, animated,
charming, varied, hundred-fold kind, just as a lively
imagination presented them; and I had, as a poet, nothing more to do than artistically to round off and elab-
orate such views and impressions and, by means of a
lifelike representation, so to bring them forward that
others might receive the same impression in hearing or
reading my representation of them"; i.e., the same impression that life itself would make on the beholder, who
was observant of its sequences of cause and effect as having unvarying results.[1]

He elsewhere calls attention to the vital difference between this method of selecting and presenting pictures of
life, and representing them as life itself, not merely as an
allegory to set forth an idea, and says: "It makes the
greatest difference, whether the poet seeks the particular
in the universal, or observes the universal in the particular. In the first method we have an allegory, where the
particular serves only as a example of the universal: but
the second method properly belongs to the nature of
poetry; that expresses the particular without thinking of
the universal, or pointing it out. Now one who vividly
seizes the particular preserves at the same time the universal therewith, without entirely perceiving it, or at
least not till afterwards." [2]

"The universal and the particular mingle together:
the particular is the universal appearing under varied

[1] *Eckermann,* May 6, 1827, pp. 258–59.
[2] *Sprueche in Prosa, Maximen und Reflexionen,* IV, *Werke,* IV,
p. 149.

conditions . . . Therefore the most individual appears always as the image and symbol of the most universal." [1]

This, then, is the method in which *Faust* was produced, viz.: a series of pictures of life in all the varied departments of the activities of existence: in the reflections of these activities the reader can trace the results of varied actions as being constantly the same. That being the case, the thoughtful observer is forced to the conclusion that the like effect must spring from a like cause, and so arrives at the central thought of the whole, viz.: that there is a universal Control of existence, exercised by the trend of the whole, and that it is a *necessity* for the individual or the race to act in accord therewith, because otherwise the individual comes into opposition to this universal, creative tendency, and is injured or thrust aside and destroyed, that the current of life be not obstructed; which last is also a necessity for the onward movement itself.

In the First Part we are shown this *Immutable Law* of life acting in the mirrored experiences of an individual. We are then shown, in the Second Part, that the destructive effect on the individual of action adverse to the general progression, the creative Control of all life, is repeated and mirrored in the destruction of a political régime not in accord with the progressive tendency of the whole. The same effect is produced from a like cause repeated and mirrored in the world of Science, in Art, and in the Church, when their activities are not in accord with the general tendency, and are not based on a clear conception of this controlling element. The pseudo-science is rejected and scoffed at, as being as unreal as necromancy; the Art is only productive of

[1] *Sprueche in Prosa, Ueber Naturwissenschaft,* IV, *Werke,* IV, p. 216.

unreal phantoms and cast contemptuously aside. The
tenets of the Church, not in accord with the facts of existence, are soon mocked at as the mummeries of a sor-
cerer; and the Church itself that is not useful to the general progression, but intent only on its own aggrandise-
ment, is denounced and overthrown.

These reflections, and re-mirrorings of a single theme,
everywhere operative in like manner, give the reader a
truly scientific basis of belief which must be incorruptible; because it is founded on observation extended not
only over all the history of Man, but is illustrated also in
all the processes of Nature itself.

Goethe said in this connection to Riemer that "there
are many of our experiences, which do not allow themselves to be completely (*rund*) and directly imparted;
I have therefore adopted the method of placing reflecting images of these experiences in opposition to each
other to exhibit their similarity to each other, and to
reveal therein their mysterious significance to the
observer." [1]

On January 31, 1823, he wrote to Professor Naeke at
Bonn to the same effect, viz.: "Now one may consider
that the repeated ethical mirrorings (*Spiegelungen*) of
the past, not only preserves them in lifelike manner;
but even exalts their significance into a revelation of a
higher existence. One thinks of this method as being
like the vision in the optical instrument; which, reflected from mirror to mirror, appears not paler, but first
rightly illuminated: thus one may arrive at a symbol of
what has constantly repeated itself and still daily repeats itself in the history of Art, Science, the Church,
and indeed in the political world." [2]   In his poem en-

[1] *Schroeer*, Vol. II, p. lxxiv.   [2] *Schroeer*, Vol. II, p. lxxv.

titled *Entoptische Farben*, Goethe also describes what he
has done in his *Faust* in placing these mirroring aspects
of life in apposition to each other, viz.: "Mirrors here,
mirrors there, a selected, duplicate arrangement; and
between these lies the being of Earth, beheld as in a
crystal. The Name [of God] becomes a symbol, with
which the crystal is profoundly penetrated. . . . Let
the spectral visions of the Macrocosm serve for what
they may be worth: since the dear little world holds
really something of the Most Glorious within itself." [1]

Goethe, as appears later, has said that we can dimly
comprehend the source of life by observing the activities
of life and their sequences and results. In his *Sayings in
Prose* he speaks of a work which exactly describes the
motif and method of his *Faust;* viz.: "To carry one on-
wards and to bring to view the significance of all being,
from the simplest to the most complex life: and so with
word and image to lay the great mystery open before the
eyes. Nothing here arises but what has already announced itself; and the announced first becomes clear
through the announcement; like the prophecy through
its fulfilment." [2]

Writing of *Faust*, Goethe said: "A dramatic author
should not dogmatise; he must note and make evident
the significance in thousands of cloaked forms, but never
be directly didactic: he must let the meaning develop
itself where it will." [3] As he said to Caroline Herder,
"the idea must be acted, not spoken." [4]

[1] *Gedichte, Entoptische Farben, Werke* ii, p. 233.
[2] *Sprueche in Prosa, Ueber Naturwissenschaft,* v, *Werke,* iv, p. 222.
[3] *Goethe to Charlotte von Stein,* April 6, 1782, *Stein, Goethes Briefe,*
ii, p. 234.
[4] July 17, 1782, *Same* ii, p. 245.

THE POET'S METHOD OF PRODUCTION

Goethe has told us that the First Part was "all drawn from his own bosom," at a time when he was in a state of "semi-darkness" as to the meaning of life.

He said elsewhere that as life in youth was not clear to him, "the First Part of *Faust* was the result of a certain darkness"; and that as life developed itself before him, he wrote this or the other scene illustrating his outlook, as he says: [1] "From the different gradients of life's pyramid," — and then later filled in the gaps.[2]

His method of composing was, when any aspect of life troubled or annoyed or interested him, to turn the subject into a poetic trope, which would appear to be something other than it really was, viz.: it would appear to be a part of the story of Dr. Faust, though it was in fact a view of the activities of life taken, in the First Part, from Goethe's personal experiences of early life, and, in the Second Part, from his estimates of the experiences of the race. "This Second Part," he tells us, "suggests the whole of antiquity and half the history of the modern world."

In a letter to Eichstadt of September 15, 1804, Goethe sets forth his method of work and the reasons for not regarding the parts separately, but for contemplating the result as a whole, as follows: —

"Every poet composes his work from elements, which one indeed, as well as another, may weave together to organise into a connected fabric, yet the principles from which these proceed will also occur to many observers.

[1] *Maskenzug 14*, December 18, 1818, *Werke*, IV, p. 318.
[2] *Graef*, p. 598.

If the beholder has a desire to separate and pull to pieces, he thus destroys, or at least lessens, that unity of the whole which the artist has striven to reach. He should rather connect than separate, and thus he will help the artist, and at the same time complete his design.

"It can be shown in the Raphael frescoes how they were carried on part by part, and how the artist was on one day more successful with his work than on another; but to do that, one must examine the work from a point near it, and yet every picture must be enjoyed from a certain distance. If some products of mechanical methods, like engravings and mosaics, exhibit themselves to the eye, when closely examined, as technical atoms, the highest effect of the work of art is quite lost.

"This method is only so far of importance that the poet, especially the living modern poet, must compose and set forth his work in such a way that it shall have a claim on the interested sympathy of his reader and critic; that they may proceed with him constructively, and do not tear to pieces delicate, possibly fragile fabric by means of a disjunctive method, or enlarge a rent already somewhat open."

It is also true of his *Faust*, as he here observes, that "much which here appears difficult of comprehension is so because I [Goethe] cannot fully carry out the uniting individual principle, because it fails in relation to absolute art, etc.: further, the disharmony appears to the poet as the earthly condition of a beautiful nature, as the human weakness of a noble soul, as the negative member of a beautiful contrast. I have often found, through rigid testing of my own and others' way of life and art, that what one may properly call a false endeavour, may be, for the individual, a round-a-bout way to the goal which he cannot forego." [1]

Goethe also says much the same thing in *Wilhelm Meister:* "If . . . I have still to confess that I can only hope to arrive at the goal of my intention by a circuitous route, what am I to say, how can I excuse myself? In any case I should have to bring forward what follows. If it is allowable to the humourist to mix up his matter in the minutest confusion, when he impudently leaves it to his reader to find out at last in half-meanings what, if anything, is to be got out of it; should it not be permitted to the intelligent and rational man to work in a method apparently as strange towards many points; so that one may at last see them reflected and concentrated in one focus, and may learn to understand how the most varied influences surrounding a man drive him to a conclusion, which he would have been able to attain in no other way, either through inward impulse or outward motive. . . . You must just possess your soul in patience and read and read on; for at last there will suddenly dawn upon you, and seem quite natural, that which, spoken in one word, would have struck you as exceedingly strange, and in fact to such a degree that you have hardly cared afterwards to give a moment to these introductions in the form of explanations." [2]

In *Faust,* as in *Wilhelm Meister,* the incidents of the story are not related for their separate interest, but as images of all the varied phases of a like manifestation of the one Controlling Power of existence, as it appears in the life of an individual and of the world at large. Goethe

[1] *Briefe,* Weimar Ausgeb., Abtheilung iv, Band 17, pp. 196–98.
[2] *Wilhelm Meister's Travels,* Book ii, Chap. xii, p. 280. *Wanderjähre,* p. 247.

saw these phases of life embodied and reflected in the ancient story of Dr. Faust, his vain aspirations, and the miseries incident to his want of accord with the vital principle of existence. He therefore retells this story, not for its own interest as a legend merely, but as such an image of the whole course and tendency of the life of an individual and of the race.

The legend is as follows: —

THE LEGEND AND THE GROWTH OF THE DRAMA

THE LEGEND

Goethe tells Zelter that the legend of Faust seems to have arisen in the sixteenth and developed itself in the seventeenth centuries.[1] This legend grew up round the life of an individual, one Johann Faust, who was born towards the close of the fifteenth century in the little town of Knittlingen, in Würtemburg, in Germany. This Faust attended the University of Cracow, where he studied magic, a regular part of the curriculum, and afterwards travelled extensively through Europe. There were various versions of his story published in the sixteenth and seventeenth centuries, and there were many dramatizations thereof, including the famous English *Dr. Faustus* of Marlowe. The popular puppet-play on the subject, Goethe tells us, was seen by him in childhood, and it made a lasting impression upon him; so that it "rang many-toned within him," when "the subject of *Faust* was first moulding itself into poetic form" in his mind, in 1770.

Goethe himself had also studied magic, medicine, law, and theology, like this old, semi-mythical, semi-histori-

[1] *Goethe to Zelter*, November 20, 1829, p. 374.

cal, famous travelling scholar; who was renowned for his skill in necromancy, crystal-gazing, and also for his achievements in medicine and other arts. This legendary Faust, like the young Goethe, as a result of his scholastic education lost his faith in a Controlling Deity; and therefore, seeing no reason to act from other motives than his personal advancement and benefit, the old necromancer gave himself over to the Devil; and made a compact with- the Fiend to secure for himself happiness in this life, with the condition that the Devil should have the right to destroy him, Faust, at the end of twenty-four years of continuous revelry.

Goethe saw in the story of this restless, grasping, old scholar, who called himself *philosophus philosophorum*, who "took to himself the wings of an eagle and would explore all the secrets of heaven and earth," an image of his own early experiences and aspirations. These he combined with the incidents and imagined results of his first love affair with the real Gretchen, his desertion of Frederica, and the attitude of Society towards the unmarried mother of his child, Christine; and he produced these incidents in the First Part of the drama of *Faust* as a trope, an image of his, Goethe's, early failure to realize the creative law of life as an individual. In this story of his Faust, he tells us, we are to see as in a mirror, a Microcosm of "that little world of folly," the life of Man, its mistakes and miseries.

In the later portions of the old Faust legend, his deluding the people by rhetoric and unreal sorceries, his riding in a chariot drawn by dragons, his attempt to call up the shade of the Grecian ideal of Beauty, the Helena, his having a child by her, his assisting the Emperor by magic arts to win the victory, Goethe saw a symbol and

image of that history of mankind, which he, by means of
these images, has embodied in the Second Part of his
Faust, as a visualization of the action of one unvarying
law of existence, active in like manner in the individual
and the race.

We are to see in Part I of the drama that the Fiend, the
spirit of selfishness, the destructive negation of the creative power of love, is the force which stirs Faust up, from
useless ruminating, to action which is necessarily creative. This action brings Faust into harmony with the
creative tendency of life; and that relieved him of the
despair which had almost driven him to suicide; a despair caused by a loss of faith, and by an inactive,
merely speculative life, of no service to the trend of the
whole of existence.

The miseries and tragedy which follow are to be observed as the result of Faust's and Margaret's failure to
continue in harmony with the controlling creative and
sustaining tendency of life, by sustaining and developing
the new-born life, which the joy of their creative love
had given them.

This is the individual experience of a universal law;
the demand of the controlling tendency of life, that the
part must function in a manner serviceable to the trend
of the whole; a law whose universality is developed in
the scenes of the Second Part, where the action mirrors
the like operation of the same tendency, manifest in all
phases of activity, as we behold them in the history of
the human race.

THE DATES OF PRODUCTION

Goethe's *Faust* was begun in 1770–73, and was taken by its author to Weimar in November, 1775, as a mass of unfinished fragments, upon which he appears to have been occupied during this year. It was read to the admiring Weimar circle; and was there copied, in its then condition, by Luise von Goechhausen, a Maid of Honour at Court; this copy was found in 1887, and published by Erich Schmidt, under the title of *Goethe's Faust in Urspruenglicher Gestalt;* an edition which is known as the *Urfaust*.

THE URFAUST

This primitive *Faust* begins with the first two hundred and fifty odd lines of the opening soliloquy and the interviews with the Earth Spirit and with Wagner; which mirror Goethe's own youthful disgust with life, occasioned by his inactivity and want of realization of the tendency and meaning of existence as *service.* This first draft has also imperfect versions of the "Scholar" and the "Cellar" scenes, afterwards much extended and altered, and has the "Gretchen" scenes substantially as they appear in the final version; but there improved and somewhat changed in regard to their position.

This *Urfaust* is probably mainly composed of such portions of the scattered mass of manuscript, which Goethe showed to Knebel in 1774, as seemed to the author worthy of preserving. Though evidently not the whole of the material already produced, it is of great importance to the student of the poem, as showing its author's method of production, and the condition of his mind; that "semi-darkness as to the meaning of life" of which he has spoken.

The omission in the *Urfaust* of all that follows in the revised and completed drama, between the first exit of Wagner and the interview between Mephistopheles and the "Student" (a name later changed to "Scholar"), leaves the reader with only the vague idea of Faust's longing to solve the problem of cause and effect in life, and of Faust's disgust with the education of the time; because its pseudo erudition failed to supply any information as to the relation of the incidents of life to the *Cause* thereof.

The imperfect prose version, in the *Urfaust*, of the "Auerbach's Cellar" scene only suggests that the life of a society given over to a vulgar self-indulgence is a delusive mode of existence; similar in its innate vulgarity to the vulgar, superstitious boors, whom the youthful Goethe had watched and scorned in his student days in Leipzig.

The "Gretchen" scenes, that follow in the *Urfaust*, appear only as a disconnected "episode," partly written in verse and partly in prose. Standing alone, without the later inserted material, introduced to call attention to their connection with the central idea, and without the "Wood and Cavern" scene, which shows the relation of their incidents to the general law of Nature, and lacking the "Walpurgis Night" scene, which connects them with the destructive trend of modern society, the incidents of this episode are but a very vivid picture of a common enough experience: the only idea originally conveyed being, the not unusual conclusion, that the selfish pursuit of pleasure is apt to victimize others and land the pursuer in remorse.

In the revised and completed version of the drama, with its two explanatory Prologues, setting forth the poet's intention, and then his view of the action of the cause and tendency of life as explaining its effects, we have the connection of the parts and their relation to the whole fully set forth and duly made evident.

Goethe tells us that all this was impossible to him at the time when the *Urfaust* was written; because the significance of life itself was not as yet clear to him, and he was still "as one walking in the twilight," along "an obscure and dusky way"; but, when he went to Rome, the whole significance of life became illuminated for him through his scientific investigations: he was then enabled to seize that "thread of Ariadne" which led him through the labyrinth of all existence, and was thus forced to make that "plan" of his drama of life anew.

After these scenes of the *Urfaust* were put together, before or near the time of Goethe's first arrival in Weimar, he was constantly occupied with the dissipated life of that Court, — a mode of life which he had satirized in the "Cellar" scene, — and with more serious affairs of State; and so had little opportunity for scientific observations or philosophical thought. He therefore did no more work on the theme of Faust, till he was granted a long vacation and sent to Italy by the Grand Duke, that he might have requisite leisure for the development of his scientific and poetical attainments.

In Rome, some fifteen years after his first Weimar experiences, he resumed his work on *Faust* and wrote the "Witch's Kitchen" scene, after coming out from a papal function in the Sistine Chapel. He then revised and arranged the whole manuscript, and made the "plan" of the drama anew. He here also acquired the material for the "Carnival" scene of the Second Part, as he looked from his window in the Corso upon the Carnival itself, and thought of it as a picture of human life.

But he seems to have done little else to the manuscript in Rome beyond writing this "Kitchen" scene, and revising and rearranging the already written portions; and, probably, writing the "Wood and Cavern" scene in 1788.[1]

In the year 1790 Goethe published such scenes of the First Part as he was then willing to give to the public, under the title of "Faust, a Fragment"; omitting the " Valentine " scene and the last three scenes, which we find in prose in the Goechhausen manuscript.

The work was then laid aside until the year 1797, when he writes to Schiller, that he "intends taking up his *Faust* again, and will, if not complete it, at least bring it a good bit further on"; and "carry out his plan, *which is as yet only an idea.*" This is the "plan" which he conceived in Rome; and, from the Prologues written in this year, we learn that the *idea* is the relation of the activities of Mankind to the Control which governs the whole of existence: to be shown, first, as the experience of an individual (Part I), and then as the similar experiences of the race (Part II).

The First Part was not, however, ready to be published till 1808, and, though he was at work on the Second Part in 1800, the latter was not finished till 1831. This completed drama (Part II) was finally published after his death, which occurred the following year.

[1] *Schroeer*, Vol. II, p. L.

THE COMPLETED DRAMA

THE RELATION AND ADAPTION OF EACH SCENE TO THAT CENTRAL IDEA, WHICH BINDS THE DIFFERENT PARTS OF THE DRAMA INTO A COMPLETED WHOLE

> "Thy song is turning like the starry vault,
> Beginning and the end are e'er the same,
> And what the middle brings is thus revealed,
> 'T is what the end and the beginning were."
> (*West-oestlicher Diwan*, II, *Hafiz*, 6, *Werke*, III, p. 30.)

THIS verse of Goethe's and the prose remark, later quoted herein, which says the same thing of *Faust*, exactly explain how we are to elucidate that poem. We have only to note that the poem begins with a statement of the guiding, controlling, life-producing, life-sustaining power of attraction exercised by "that highest manifestation of the Creative," *Die Sonne* (the Sun, in German is a feminine not a masculine power), and we have to observe that the poem ends with the remark; that all the events related are the symbols of this Creative Force, there described as *Das Ewig-weibliche*: To understand all that lies between these we have then to regard every incident as a manifestation, first, in the life of an individual (Part I), and then in the life of the race (Part II), of the control exercised by this Creative Power of Attraction, and the necessity for the part to function in harmony therewith.

So regarded, the connection of the so-called "love episode" of the First Part, with this drama of life as a whole is then evident: not as merely an episode, but as an individual experience of the operation of the universal law, which is seen to be the theme of the whole.

THE FIRST PART

When Goethe "revised and adapted every smallest part" to set forth the idea of the whole, he prepared the two Prologues thereunto, that he printed with the First Part of the tragedy; which Part exhibits those life-experiences of an individual, who, he has told us, is himself.

The "Prologue in the Theatre" sets forth, through the mouth of *The Poet*, the author's intention and method in writing this drama. This *Poet* there says that his intention is not the *Manager's* notion of a play to make money and draw the crowd, nor the *Jovial Personage's* idea of a drama to merely entertain the audience. We, however, must remember that Goethe said elsewhere, it was necessary to include these elements, if the writer would collect an audience and hold the attention of the hearers he wished to instruct: this is a sufficient reason for the embodiment of his philosophy in a poetic, dramatic form.

The *Poet* then tells us that his real intention is to "call" the individual life to act in harmony (*in herrlichen accorden schlaegt*) with the universal dedication (*allgemeinen Weihe*) of the whole of life to one end: viz.: the "universal evolution into something higher and better." He further promises that he will herein assure us of the existence of an all-controlling Power dedicated to this end (*sichert den Olymp*), and of the essential unity of all religious views which set forth the idea of this Power as the creative, controlling God (*vereinet Goetter*).

The Prologue in Heaven calls attention to what we can observe in the Universe about and above us of the existence of such a Control; here visualized as the controlling "Lord." We are first asked to observe the effect of this control as exercised by *Die Sonne* (*N.B.*, a feminine, not a masculine force) by means of *her* power of attraction, which holds *her* brother-spheres, the planets, on their course, and to note that the destructive lightnings are the "messengers" (*Boten*) of this "Almighty Lord." They clear the path for the "calm progression" (*sanfte Wandeln*) of His Day."

Mephistopheles, the embodiment of all the destructive agencies, evils, delusions, and miseries that afflict mankind, then appears as also among the train of followers who are *serviceable* to the controlling Power. This "Lord" tells this mocking Spirit of Negation, that Faust, the image of man, is also his, the Lord's, "Servant"; and that his, the Lord's, pathway, this calm, creative evolution of life, is the "one right way" for Faust to follow. This "Lord" also points out the usefulness of this Mephistopheles, the destructive tendencies of life, in stirring man up to action in accord with this controlling, creative movement.

This, then, is the *motif* of the drama, succinctly stated: the idea which binds the varied scenes together. It is the "clue of Ariadne," that Goethe found while in Rome, and which, he has told us, will lead us through the labyrinth of life, represented in these scenes as the separate images of one universal law.

To understand this drama of life we have, then, only to grasp this central idea, that there is such a Control of existence, visible in the Solar system as the Power of Attraction of the feminine Sun; a Power which holds the units of life upon their preordained course, creates life, sustains it, and brings it on to higher development. Goethe would show us, in the incidents and sequences of life around us, a like manifestation of this same Power of Attraction, as also "dedicated" to the same end. He points out that we can observe an exactly similar action of this Power, in the effect of the attraction of Beauty in Woman, whose creative action is like that of the "highest manifestation" of this Power of Control which we observe in the Sun; in that woman likewise gives herself warmly forth, not only to propagate life, but also to sustain it and promote its development.

The theme of the drama is then the theme of Faust's meditations in the first scene, viz.: what can we know of the Source of Existence, its control over life, and the effect of the apparently destructive evils as an integral part of the action of this Control? We are throughout to see this idea; and to note how each scene is related thereunto, and tends to develop this underlying theme of the whole.

We must also always keep in mind the fact that the scenes of the First Part are nearly all drawn from the Poet's own personal experiences of this universal tendency or law of all existence; and that those of the Second Part are his observations of the similar effect of the like tendency in all phases of human activity.

This theme of the drama is developed by a series of contrasts between the lives or actions not in harmony with this controlling dedication of all life; and those which act in accord therewith (*in herrlichen Accorden schlaegt*). The lives not so in accord are shown to be

miserable and tending towards self-destruction: the lives
which act in harmony with this controlling Principle of
life and have a direct faith therein — under conventional
forms of belief or otherwise — are exhibited as full of
happiness which springs from such accord.

This comparison is evident in the first two scenes: the
earlier written first scene, describing the effect of such a
want of belief as the failure of all the erudition of the
time to supply an adequate reason for belief in this control and for action in accord therewith; and the second
scene, interpolated after Goethe had himself realized
this law of life and the *rationale* of its action, which
scene sets forth the happiness incident to such belief
and to action in accord therewith.

The first scene, *Night*, "the high-vaulted, narrow
Gothic chamber," opens with Faust's lament that all the
erudition of his time has left him "no wiser than before";
i.e., on this all-important point of the existence of such a
controlling Source of Life, nor of the relations of the
parts of life thereunto. He had therefore lost all faith,
and has neither "scruple nor doubt, nor is afraid of Hell
nor Devil": but (*N.B.*) from this very cause (*Dafuer*),
"every joy is torn away from him"; and when he tries to
arrive at the Source of Life through the arts of necromancy, he only succeeds in bringing up before him a
vague "awful spectre," "The Earth Spirit," who says
Faust cannot understand him. Later the priest and the
astrologer are classed together; and herein we have the
suggestion of the impossibility of solving the problem of
life by any magic of the imagination, or process of metaphysical speculation: really to know anything of the subject we must study its action in the effects on our own
life, and on the race. Faust's efforts to solve the problem

by futile speculation about it, instead of studying it in
life itself, have only led him into doubt of the existence
of any Control exercised over life, and brought him
to the verge of self-destruction; from whence he is
saved by hearing the songs of the faithful outside the
study.

We are to note that his life of idle, unproductive speculation about life, having no connection with life itself,
is unserviceable; and the resulting doubt of the existence
of any Control exercised over life, leads him to a suicidal
mania: a tendency now prevalent in the modern world,
from a like disbelief in a Power that demands service of
man, and from the consequent loss of scruple in the pursuit of happiness or gain. It is a materialism, which
brought the same mania into the antique world, and
which led to the destruction of antique civilizations.

The second scene, *Outside the Gate*, sharply empha-
sizes the contrast between the misery of the doubt-
ing empiric philosopher, leading a useless life of idle,
false speculation, not based on any observation of life
itself, and the abounding joy of the creative, happy
workers whose lives are serviceable to the controlling
tendency of life: they enjoy themselves because they are
in accord with this tendency; which they adore and
worship as the creative God, and as the joy of the risen
Christ, whose life was an example of submission to the
Creator's will. This happiness springs from union with
the Creative, and is the result of such harmony between
the functioning of the individual part of life, and the
functioning of the environment, the controlling, creative tendency of the whole. The happiness, which
springs from this union with the Divine Control, is characterized, in the Disciple's song closing the first scene, as

the *Schaffender Freude;* as that creative joy which is a manifestation of the Creative Power.

Towards the close of the second scene, Faust observes the attractive action of "that highest manifestation of the creative," the Sun; and refers to it as the attraction of a "Goddess"; (*N.B.*) *not a God.* We must again recall that the whole theme of the drama is the force of this feminine Creative Attraction, which is omnipotent and present in all existence.

Here, in contact with Nature, Faust feels this life-creating Power of Attraction; but, at the pedant Wagner's suggestion, he turns away from Nature and goes back to that futile "Study-Chamber"; taking with him the "black dog" who is an "excellent scholar of the Students"; like them, he learns his tricks by rote.

Scene III. *The Study-Chamber.* Shut away from Nature in the "Study," Faust returns to his speculations about the Source of Life, its "beginning"; and finds only the metaphysical statement, that the "beginning was the Word." That does not enlighten him, and he states the Goethean conclusion, that we must look at the "Deed," i.e., at the action of life itself, if we would know anything of the Source. The "black dog" objects and assumes the aspect of the theological description of the Devil. Faust confronts this other horrible, vague "Spectre" with the "Four Elements of Nature," and finds nothing in them of this "Beast"; he compares this horrible vision with the Christ-life, as a revelation of the Deity, "diffused through all heaven"; then the "mist falls" and reveals this destructive, evil Demon as merely a figment of scholastic imagination; he is a "travelling scholasticus." That is, the theological Devil opposed to the Good Lord is a vague spectre, evolved by metaphysical lucubrations to account for the presence of "sin, destruction, the evil": but *Mephistopheles*, speaking as *Chorus* to declare the real intention of the author, calls attention to the fact that though he seems "to will the evil, he does the good."

This is the relation of the scene to the main theme, the absolute, unconditioned control over all action of "the Power which makes for righteousness." As the apparent Demon of Denial and Doubt, this Devil does the good by stirring men up to solve the problem of life for themselves; as the Evil and Sin which lead to destruction, he clears the pathway of the controlling Power of Development of all unserviceable hindrances to this beneficent progress: as The Tempter, he *tests* Man (*N.B.*) to prove his fitness for service to this Progression.

All these phases of the destructive action of the Power which works all things for the ultimate good of the whole are embodied in this figure of Mephistopheles; who seems to be opposed to the good "Lord" of the Prologue; but who appears there as one among his train of *servants*. We note now that the Demon of Doubt got into the "Study" because the "pentagram," "the Witch's footprint," on the sill "was not well drawn": the "outer side" (i.e., the side toward Nature outside the study) was "open."

This pentagram is a figure of three triangles combined in a single star, emblematic of the theological exposition of the Source of Life as a triune Deity, three persons and yet one personality. In the "Witch's Kitchen" scene, Faust expresses Goethe's dislike of this involved metaphysical idea, as being a thing imported into Christianity from "beyond the sea"; difficult of

comprehension, and therefore tending to admit doubt
of the existence of the Deity into the mind.

As the Tempter, Mephistopheles fills Faust's mind
with a vision of beautiful forms and lovely women and
their lovers in verdant bowers. These lovers are described as "children of Heaven"; i.e., they obey the
creative instinct. The effect of this tempting vision is to
lead Faust in the next scene away from useless speculation out into active participation with life.

The fourth scene, *Study-Chamber*, next following,
shows us this effect; and includes a disquisition on the
academic learning of the time, by Mephistopheles dis-
guised in a professor's cap and gown, which he finds a
"precious fit." This discussion is with a "Scholar";
note the word which suggests in German a scholastic person, for which reason it was changed by Goethe from the
word "Student," when the drama was revised by him.
This portion of the scene is a review of the scholastic
education of the time, as failing to convey any real
information as to the Source of Life, or the relation of the
parts thereof, to the controlling tendency of the whole.

> "He has the parts then in his hand
> But lacks, alas! the spirit's band."
> *Faust*, I, lines 1938–39.

Faust then goes out of the "Study" to "experience what
life may be," with no idea of the relation of the parts of
life to its controlling Source. He is tired to death of
the miserable, useless life he has led, and sells himself to
the Destructive, if this Demon can give him "a moment of happiness." The quest is then "the pursuit of
happiness": we are to see the effect of such a course
of action in the incidents that follow.

The *Auerbach's Cellar*, Scene v, at first only imaged

Goethe's disgust with a life given up to guzzling and low amusements, as he observed this "pursuit of happiness" in Leipzig and Weimar: a course of life which ended in cutting off the roysterer's own nose.' He later saw in this unserviceable mode of life another evidence of the effect of a loss of belief in the control exercised by that *Causa Finalis* of life, and gave the delusive tricks to Mephistopheles, instead of to Faust, as originally written, and inserted some lines suggestive of the ideas of the "Apostles of Freedom" of the French Revolution. He bids us observe that "this time" the "Hellfire," which flames up, is really "only a drop of Purgatory fire," a "friendly Element"; in the Second Part we shall see in the conflagration that follows a like foolery in the world-society another instance of the good arising from the apparent evil.

The *Witch's Kitchen*, Scene VI, was written in Rome just after Goethe had come out into the "freer air" from witnessing a papal function, on which he had "made his quiet observations." It mirrors that "Protestant revulsion," which he said he felt in coming in contact with ceremonial Romanism; when he "could not help shuddering to think of the shapeless, not to say grotesque, mass of heathenism, which heavily over-lays the benign beginnings of original Christianity." He says that "under the form of ugly, ridiculous figures, which seem to be absurd things, he sets forth the highest thought."

This thought is again the futility of metaphysical expositions of the *Causa Finalis*, and the falsity of dismal views of life. He, however, recognizes, that ceremonies, which seem to be merely superstitious mummeries, are really a poetic setting forth of a profound idea. Mephistopheles says: "We must at least admit that these absurd creatures are genuine poets."

The scene sets forth the emotional result of religious ceremonies, as stirring the whole emotional nature into action, and thus forwarding the procreative function. This is imagined here as the rejuvenating potion in the Witch's chalice, over which flicker little flames of Hell; a suggestion of part of the relation of this scene to the main theme.

This scene also contains an eloquent tribute to the reality of the Church's image of the "Mother of God"; an image which Goethe uses at the conclusion of the drama as the *Mater Gloriosa;* a visualization of what we can perceive in life of the action of the Creative Power: there, and here, represented as

> "*an epitome of all the heavens.*"

The rest of the drama is taken up by the so-called Gretchen episode; which is really an integral part of the whole theme, inasmuch as it is a setting forth of the relation of the reproductive instinct to the control of life exercised by that *Causa Finalis;* which Goethe would show us is peculiarly manifested in the procreative function of Love, the visible source of all present existence.

In the first scene of this part of the drama (Scene VII, *Street*) Faust feels the power of that irresistible attraction of Beauty, to which all life owes its continuance. Having lost all faith in a Control of life, and therefore believing in the "pursuit of happiness" as one of the "Rights of Man," Faust only desires to possess this Beauty as a means of personal enjoyment; and sets Mephistopheles — who has indoctrinated him with this false theory of life — to work to accomplish his desires.

In the next scene (VIII, *Evening*) we have the suggestion of Love as an elevating, purifying force that "draws us upward and onward." In his *Sayings in Prose* Goethe calls attention to the "relation of desire to productivity and to that love of the Divine which ever strives towards the highest." The little chamber is a *Heiligthum*, a shrine filled with the atmosphere of this "heavenly girl"; whose serviceable existence of simple usefulness and devout aspiration is to Faust a *Goetter-bild*, an image of the Deity. Her creative, sustaining hand is like the action of The Divine, (*Goettergleich*); through her presence the cottage becomes a "heavenly realm" (*Himmelreich*). The beautiful, devoted, actively-useful, self-renouncing woman, ever giving forth self in creative, sustaining activity, is that image of the Creative, which is the theme of the drama.

The next scene (IX, *A Pleasure Walk*) contrasts the pious, good woman, suspicious of the destructiveness of unearned benefits, with the greed of the Church, which has "eaten up whole countries."

Scene X, *The Neighbour's House*, contrasts the woman whose life is a destructive pursuit of happiness, to which she desecrates the creative function, with the life of the simple girl who is pious and good, and useful to the great creative progression of all life. The corruption of Margaret begins with the acceptance of possessions which she has not earned. Faust said: "To possess anything we must first earn it." Mephistopheles recounts the useless life of pleasure led by "Herr Schwertlein," and recalls the theme of the drama in his remark: —

"Yes, see! For that he now is dead."

Scene XI, *The Street*, seems to be introduced to show

the result of false definitions of the creative power; and
to account for the baseness of Faust's action, as the
effect of his being drawn with an irresistible force into
the ultimate catastrophe by that "one-everywhere-
almighty-creative-impulse"; which tests all things to
prove their fitness for accord with the creative, sustaining tendency of life.

Mephistopheles herein alludes to the inadequacy of
University teaching, previously suggested, as a "bearing
of false witness," concerning God, the World, and what
"therein bestirs itself."

The famous *Garden* scene (XII) again contrasts
the innate vulgarity of lives given up to mere pleas-
ure-seeking, with the true nobility of those simple,
good, industrious, creative members of what, as Goethe
said, "are called the lower classes; but which, in the
sight of God, are certainly the highest." Of the so-called
higher class of women, Goethe remarked: "It is incon-
ceiveable how lowering the intercourse with such women
is . . . they may be without any consequence or plan,
except to play a rôle, live and enjoy; yet they ruin every
domesticity into which they enter." In these figures of
Martha, the pander, who wants to join her life with
Mephistopheles, the Destructive, and Margaret, the
simple, useful, devout, and devoted girl of the people,
whom we have seen represented as the image of the creative Power, we have again the suggestion of the theme
of the whole drama, the action of the creative and destructive forces.

The short scene connected with this (XIII, *The Sum-
mer House*) recalls an incident of the Frederica episode,
as that is related in the *Autobiography*.

The next scene (XIV, *Wood and Cavern*) was written

in Rome, after Goethe's scientific studies had en-
lightened him further as to the Source of life, and the
control exercised thereby over all phases of existence.
The relation of this scene to the motive of the whole
drama consists in its calling attention to the universality
of the creative and destructive tendencies, and the irresistibleness of the procreative power of life, as everywhere operative in like manner; in plants, in animals,
and in man. The "Spirit Sublime" here: —

> "leadest the series of the Living, past
> Before me, teachest me to know my brothers
> In silent underwoods, in air and water."

Writing to Knebel of his discovery of the intermaxil-
lar bone, Goethe speaks of its proof of "the near kinship
of men and animals; and of each as a part, a tone in a
universal harmony."

Mephistopheles, who is the friend of the Witch, and
who masqueraded in the professor's cap and gown, sneers
at these "mysterious miracles" revealed in the study of
Nature; he brings us the vulgar idea of this all-controlling Love, as merely the pursuit of pleasure, and here
reminds Faust that the life of idle speculation had nearly
led Faust to suicide. He tells Faust that Margaret, too,
is singing an old folk-song, expressing the ungovernable
desire of the beloved for the distant lover. The irresistibleness of this creative force is again set forth in Faust's
wild lament to Mephistopheles, that he must continue in
this "hellish sacrifice."

Scene xv, *Gretchen at the Spinning Wheel*, whose
beautiful simplicity is the despair of translators, empha-
sizes the irresistibleness of the creative power.

In the next scene (xvi, *Martha's Garden*) we have
the passage which has been described as Goethe's

Credo. In it Faust tells Margaret that he "will rob no one of his Church and sentiment." He tells her he "honours the Holy Sacraments"; and, when she asks him if he believes in God, he says he believes in a Power that includes all, and upholds and sustains all, and bids her: —

> "Then name it as you will:
> Name 't Bliss! Heart! Love! God!
> . . . .
> Name is but sound and smoke
> Clouding the glow of Heaven."

Margaret's objection, that, though "that sounds indeed fair and good," it cannot be right, "because Faust has no Christianity," echoes the objections that were made to Goethe's religious belief in his lifetime; but Goethe reverenced the Christ-life, as a revelation of that perfect harmony of a life which would renounce all else to give oneself forth to do The Father's Will. This is an accord which mirrors The Creative, as we can perceive its action in that "highest manifestation," the Sun; and Goethe would suggest that wherever we see this giving forth of self, this self-surrender to forward the creative progression of life, we see The Creator. This, he says, "is what stirs us in the relation of any noble self-sacrificing deed"; it is in accord with the action which we recognize as manifesting The Creative. Thus the self-sacrificing, creative love of an innocent woman, who obeys the mandate of Nature and gives herself forth creatively from an instinct of obedience, *not as a desire for her personal pleasure,* is, in this view, a thing to reverence.

Margaret feels this irresistible creative Power and obeys; though she does not understand "what drives her on to do her lover's will." Faust recognizes and rever-

ences her motive, and herein we have the relation of this
scene to the theme of the drama.

Mephistopheles, the Destructive, scoffs at this reverence, as the delusion of "a sensual, supersensual lover."
The following scenes exhibit the destructive effect of a
point of view which fails to grasp these realities of this
law of existence; and Faust here characterizes Mephistopheles' idea, as an "abortion full of filth and fire."

Scene XVII, *At the Fountain*, gives us the ordinary
point of view of the unmarried mother, as that of the
vulgar, gossiping girls in the market-place; and this was
the attitude of Weimar society towards Christine, the,
as yet, unmarried mother of Goethe's child.

Margaret, crushed by their scorn, reminds us that

> "Yet — everything that *drove* me here,
> God! was so good. Ah! was so dear."

Goethe in several of his poems bids us "not to judge so
strenuously"; and, in the *Neue Heilige* ("New Saint"),
he calls upon us to "see the Mother-love, the tears, her
remorse and sufferings," and reminds us that "we all
need *misericordias*."

Scene XVIII, *Zwinger*, the narrow covered passage
between the fetid town and the open nature outside,
presents that figure of the pitying Mother of God, which
is used in the final scene as the image of what we can con-
ceive of the Creative. We see also the tears, the remorse and heart-breaking sufferings of Gretchen, this
victim of Faust's imperfect realization of the law of the
Creative; the Law that life is *not* a pursuit of happiness,
but a demand for serviceableness to the progression of
the whole.

Scene XIX, *Street before Margaret's Door*, suggests

the destructiveness of Faust's mistaken course of life,
and contrasts the sacred figure of the previous scene
with the attitude of the man in the street, the soldier
conscious only of what he calls his "honour": to note
this contrast the light of that "Sacristy" glimmers
over the scene. The combat with the accusing soldier
brother recalls to mind the attacks on Goethe and the
unmarried mother of his child, by the Weimar society,
at the time when this scene was extended and revised.

Scene xx, *Cathedral,* repeats the pitiless anathema of
the Church, the *Dies irae;* part of which is paraphrased
and put into the mouth of the "Evil Spirit" in the
Church; who torments the unfortunate Gretchen with
the Church's vision of endless, vengeful torments: an
idea which Goethe combats in the conclusion of the
Second Part, as a theatrical device to frighten sinners: it
is wholly in disaccord with the Church's own premise,
and with what can be observed in Nature of the Creative
as a God of love.

Scene xxi, *The Walpurgis Night's Orgy in the Palace of Mammon,* contrasts again the real life of that
Society,—which traduces and vilifies the unfortunate,—
with the vision of the Creative glimpsed in the preceding
scenes, the "Zwinger" and the "Sacristy in the Street."
It was written when Goethe first came into contact with
what he called that "wild orgy of getting and spending
in our great towns," and was first deeply impressed with
the fact that "riches and rapidity" were the only things
that the citizens strove for or cared for.

It is a vision of the universal effect of materialism, and
a false pursuit of happiness, which infects a world that
has lost faith in any Controlling Power; the innate vulgarity and ruthless destructiveness of such a course of

life: to emphasize again the contrast we see, glimmering through its flaming mists, a wraith of that poor, lost child, Gretchen, who "slowly seems to move with fettered feet."

Portraits of Goethe's opponents also appear therein, whose significance as an answer to the attacks on himself will not be lost on the thoughtful reader.

Scene xxii, the fairy interlude entitled *Walpurgis Night's Dream*, is explained by a remark of the "Northern Artist," — admittedly Goethe himself, — who referred "to his inheritance (Part i) as a northern artist." It is, as this character states, "a sort of sketching merely" of what we are to see, in Part ii, of the unrealities in all forms of human activities, artistic, literary, theological, philosophical, and political, as being the result of a dilletantism; which springs from a belief that something real can be created by a method out of harmony with the Creative; a self-seeking, not a devoted giving forth of self to creative work in these fields.

So regarded, its relation to the theme of the whole is evident; it foretells what is to follow in considering this law of existence in the world-story of the Second Part; though it is introduced here, as Faust says to Mephistopheles in the next scene, as merely "an insipid, tasteless dissipation" to turn Faust's attention from his duty to the Creative, the sustaining of the mother of his child, and the new-born life their love had given them.

Incidentally it is interesting to note that many of the characters introduced to illustrate the theme are unflattering portraits of Goethe's personal opponents: originally produced for the purpose only of satirizing these individuals; but here included as individual instances of the universal effect, in all departments of hu-

man activity, of a want of accord with the creative
method.

Scene XXIII, *Gloomy Day — Field*, appears in the
Urfaust, and is only very slightly altered to fit it more
closely to the scheme of the rhythmic movement of
the prose. It is a tremendous denunciation of the
society that attacked Gretchen, and is probably the
result of that original outrage to his feelings; when the
real Gretchen, his earliest love, was attacked and forci-
bly separated from the youthful Goethe; at which time,
as he tells us in the *Autobiography*, his "whole inventive
faculty, his poetry and rhetoric flung themselves" into
this conflict on her behalf. It mirrors as well his later
wrath at the attack on Christine; and its relation to the
theme of the whole consists in the fact, that it illustrates
the destructiveness of such an attitude of a society, like
that described in the previous Walpurgis Mammon
Orgy, towards the unmarried mother and her creative
love.

The short scene (XXIV) representing the *Witch's
Guild* of ghouls around the place of execution, continues
and deepens the characterization of such a destructive
society.

In the final scene of the First Part (XXV, *Prison*),
the deaths of Margaret and of her mother, brother, and
child, show us the fatal culmination of the destructive
effect of the false idea of the "right to the pursuit of
happiness," arising from a want of comprehension of the
Control exercised on life, the necessity of accord therewith, and the result of the attitude of society towards the
unmarried mother.

It is of the earliest invention of the poet and may owe
its dramatic intensity to that "remorse," which he tells

us he felt for his desertion of Frederica, and incorporated
in several works as "a poetical confession"; or it may be
the "inevitable tragical catastrophe" which he imagined as the result of his separation from the real Gretchen.
We must, however, note that, when he revised the scene
as it stood in the prose version of the *Urfaust*, it became
to Faust a picture of the "whole misery of mankind"
(*Der Menscheits ganzer Jammer*); and that the

"Voice (*from above*). Is saved!" —

was then added.

It is Mephistopheles, the leader of that society scram-
bling upward to the Palace of Mammon, who says she
"is judged": Margaret declines her freedom because, as
she says, it would be impossible for her to live with these
destructive people, who would hound her as her dying
brother foretold.

In the last scene of the Second Part, we see the "immortal part" of Gretchen, surrounded by those "Holy
Hosts"; which she here calls upon to "camp around and
guard her," since she has put herself again fully into
accord with the Creative by voluntarily surrendering
her mortal life to the "Judgment of God." By this final
act of self-renunciation she becomes immortal; as the influence, more active after mortal dissolution, which shall
lead her lover ever upward and onward to new activities
in accord with the Control, that forever gives Itself forth
for the forwarding of all life into something higher and
better.

We have to note well that the tragedies and miseries
related came to the hero and heroine as the result of that
"pursuit of happiness," falsely declared by the philosophers to be one of the "Rights of Man," and as the

result, in the case of the heroine, of a direct action opposed to the creative action of the Love, that had given ᴇ new life into her care to sustain and bring forward to higher development.

Faust is plunged in remorse: Margaret is overwhelmed by the Current of Life, which she has actively resisted by destroying her child from fear of the effect upon herself of her creative action; the social censure which would render her continuance in that wretched mortal life insupportable.

To understand the real significance of the First Part, it is necessary to have some adequate idea of what thereafter follows; because therein the explanation of the incidents of the First Part lies, as being the individual instances of the operation of the same forces which have ever controlled all the activities of life.

Goethe said to Boisserée, that "the relation with women alone cannot entirely exhibit life"; and to Eckermann the same thing, adding that it was necessary, therefore, to complete this drama with Part II.[1]

THE SECOND PART

"The history of the race for three thousand years."

"The life of the individual is forever the mirror of the life of mankind."

(GOETHE.)

The Second Part reviews the history of the race, as showing the same destructive delusions, and failure to act in accord with the Creative, which we were asked to

---

[1] *Biedermann*, III, October 3, 1815, No. 666, p. 274.

observe in the previous life of the individual. Here we are to note, that, in all departments of human activity, this failure has arisen from the same reason; the want of a clear comprehension of the "one right way" of life; because Mankind has not directly observed the workings of all existence; but has drawn his conclusions from metaphysical speculations that have no direct relation to life itself.

The Second Part of *Faust* opens with a musical prelude, which shows us the figure of Faust as an individual suffering the torments of remorse for the destructiveness caused by his leaving that "one right way" of action serviceable to the creative tendency of life.

The fine passage concerning the sunrise, which directly follows, reminds us of Goethe's remark that he "was like a man walking in the twilight of dawn, until the idea of the immanence of Deity in all things shone upon him, and illuminated his way through the labyrinth of life." To illustrate this thought we have again the figure of that "highest manifestation of the Creative, the Sun," uprising as the glorious "Goddess," whose direct radiance blinds us, so that we are "fain to hide ourselves beneath that youthful incense-veil" of the conventional idea of Deity.

Faust then turns his back upon this refulgent spectacle, and sees the many-coloured reflection of this Controlling Power in the pouring cataract of the ages. Herein the whole theme of the Second Part is suggested. We are to see the image of the creative action in all the manifold phases of human productivity. The events hereinafter related suggest the history of mankind, as a series of pictures of all departments of human activity, reflecting the operation of the control exercised by that

universal tendency of development to which all life owes
its being, and, therefore, its allegiance.

"In this reflected glory we've *The Life*."

In Act I of this Second Part we are shown the operation of an unproductive, destructive, and therefore self-
destructive tendency of a political régime, that fails to
recognize the law of life, the reality of its Control: therefore, like the revellers in Part First, this régime gives
itself over to a destructive course of the pursuit of happiness, which is unproductive and destructive; it is a
pursuit of pleasure, a course of life similar to that pursued by the revellers and the hero of Part First.

Incidentally it is suggested that the same unreal delusion is to be seen in the monetary world, which strives to
produce a value by an unserviceable paper currency,
that represents no real thing, and has no value in itself.
It is a delusion that something can be produced from nothing, like the similar delusion of the "Auerbach's Cellar" scene; a table-trick, not a reality.

In the scene called the "Dark Gallery" we have set
forth the delusion that any Art, whose aim is merely
amusement, can be creative. Goethe regards Beauty as
an integral part of the creative attraction, the Mother-
Element, which is the controlling, creative Power. This
"criticism of life," given Faust by the great critic
Mephistopheles, is that "golden key" of life, which
leads Faust to "The Mothers"; the goddesses who have
produced all things that were.

Mephistopheles directly warns us that here he is not
speaking as the Liar; but is telling an absolute truth.
We must, however, note that the aim which leads to the
action is not in accord with this truth. The aim of

Faust in this scene is not an adoring service to the creative Power; but merely an attempt to produce an image
of the Helena as an amusement for a frivolous society.
The result is a phantom image, not a reality. It stands
in relation to the really creative Greek Art, as the
French classical drama is related to the great Greek
dramatic productions. Goethe observed that Greek dramatic art was the result of a religious devotion, imaged
in the tripod, a religious object which was the Greek
poet's reward.

The phantom-like apparition which Faust produces
for the amusement of this society, the moment it is
touched with this "golden key" (i.e., brought to this
test of reality) disappears like the disaccordant, unserviceable society itself in an explosion.

The art, that would create an ideal of beauty, must
not merely copy the dead past, or have for its aim a
self-seeking motive; but must come into contact with
life itself, and obey that creative law of life, which is the
adoring giving forth of self to accord with the creative
action.

ACT II

The subject of Act II is, as one of the characters remarks, "both old and new." It deals with the delusive
hypotheses, the dogmatism and quarrels in the realm of
Science, as being a desert waste, like the "desert waste
of robber-baronage and priestcraft of the Dark Ages";
to which the scientific world of Goethe's day, its delusions and quarrels and its unrealities, are herein com-
pared.

Its relation to the First Part consists in the suggestion, that the condition in which we found Faust and

Wagner, shut up in their *museum* of mouldy bones and
dead specimens, with no connection with life itself or its
creative source, is typical of the condition of the scientific
world at that time.

To make this evident, we are first introduced to
Faust's old Gothic study, where everything remains
"unchanged."

Here we find Wagner, that type of the merely erudite
person, engaged in that mediæval delusion, which lasted
down even to Goethe's own time, that a living human
being could be made by a process of crystallization, with
no reference to the Mother-Element. The result of such
a course of unreal erudition is, not a capable, active man,
but an Homunculus shut away from direct contact with
life, as the Wagner of the First Part was shut away from
observation of life in his "museum." The similarity
between the individual case of the First Part and this
like result on the World-Stage, explains both the image
here used, and the state of mind of the individual of the
earlier portion of the drama.

In the First Part, the individual Faust was tempted
out of the confining study by a dream of the attractive
power of Beauty; here this World-Faust, mankind, feels
the like attraction of beauty, and dreams of the relation
of the attraction of womanly beauty to the Creative
Power, as the union of Leda, the mortal, beautiful woman, and the Swan, the all-creative Zeus, Father of
gods and men; a figure which Faust owes to this scholastic mind, Homunculus, shut away from life in his glass
cell, from whence he here relates that ancient myth.

This World-Faust, illuminated by some gleams of
light from the imprisoned Homunculus, that child of
erudition in his cloistered cell, wanders through the

darkness of the warring ages searching for the Helena, the lost beauty of the Grecian civilization.

These Dark Ages of warring priestcraft and robber-baronage are represented as another Walpurgis Night: an orgy of selfishness and unreality. The figures introduced, to image the events of the time, are drawn from Grecian mythology: the scene is therefore entitled the "Classical Walpurgis Night"; that night of the Dark Ages, when classical knowledge only illuminated some monkish cells. Erichtho, who acts as *Chorus*, opening the scene, warns us that it is all a "great example" of the world-wide miseries incident to a universal course of unrealities and self-seeking, so totally at variance with that "one right way" which is the creative giving forth of self. Amid these warrings, robbings and delusions, Faust sees again that union of womanhood and the Creative, the legend of Leda repeated to emphasize the central thought of the influence of woman on civilization.

Faust is in search of the Helena, the beauty of Hellenic civilization: he now first hears of her from Chiron, the horse-man, the image of the knight-errant. Though the impelling motive of the knight-errant was often only selfish, his professed ideal was in accord with the Creative, in that it was an ideal of service to and adoration of his Queen of Beauty, and of service to his Lord and to the weak and oppressed. The Crusading knights, at least ostensibly, fought for their Lady, the Church: though the impelling incentive was self-gratification, — like the impulse which led the individual Faust in the First Part towards Margaret, — the ideal of chivalry was in accord with the creative law of life, and brought man out into the light of modern civilization.

The return of that darkened world to the brightness of
the gorgeous pageant of the Renaissance, — when men's
minds were freed from vain pedantry and reilluminated
by the humanities and the classics, — is imaged as a
festival of the sea, the triumph of that representative of
the foam-born Aphrodite, Galatea, sometimes wor-
shipped in place of the Goddess of Love. Homunculus,
this prisoned mind of man, this product of a false erudition, here shatters his confining glass cell on the sea-shell
throne of this Goddess of Love and Beauty; as the individual Faust got rid of his philosophical crotchets about
life and came out of his shell into the creative stream of
life, when he felt the feminine Power of Attraction, active
in the beauty and love of the individual woman, Margaret. This is another instance of the truth of Goethe's
remark: "that the life of the individual is forever the
mirror of the life of Man": the First Part announces
what we are to see in this history of mankind.

The main theme of the Act is somewhat obscured by
the complication introduced in the constant allusion to
the forgotten quarrels of the advocates of the Volcanic
and Neptunian theories of the creation of the earth.
To Goethe's mind these now obsolete discussions were
illustrations of his main thesis, the unserviceable destructiveness of any speculation about life not based on
direct observations of life itself; and these allusions were
therefore introduced, regardless of their obscuring effect
in taking the thought of the reader away from the main
idea.

ACT III

Act III, *The Helena*, opens with the return of these
crusading pirates and warriors to Greece, the homeland

of civilization, whose palace of Hellenic art is presided
over by this representative of Hellenic culture and of
feminine grace and beauty, the "Helena." The verse
measures are Grecian, and call attention to the thought
of that Grecian civilization as the Mother of all the Arts
and Sciences. The whole subject of Grecian art and civilization, as the result of a self-sacrificing devotion of the
individual to the forwarding of the whole race, is suggested. It is an Arcadia, but (*N.B.*)

"Arcadia in Sparta's neighbourhood."

The loss of this Arcadian civilization, it is suggested,
was due to the race having left that "one right way" of
devoted giving forth of self, to become piratical warriors;
the "Helena" is threatened by her piratical husband
with complete extinction. The return of this glorious
being to earth again, that new birth of the Renaissance,
is here again imaged: it appears this time as a mediæval
pageant of chivalry in the castle of the Northern Knight,
who speaks in the verse measures of modern poetry, and
lays all his treasures at the feet of this resplendent
Queen. It has been often remarked by the most compe-
tent judges that all which we most prize in Roman and
modern literature is directly inspired by Greek originals;
a suggestion also made by Goethe.

From the union of these representatives of the Classic
and Romantic strains, that fanciful, flighty child,
Euphorion, is born; who, Goethe has told us, "is modern
poetry." This child is a fantastic being who gambols and
leaps and springs, and finally, hearing the trumpet of
war, he falls to earth in attempting to fly; though he has
been warned by his parents to "touch the firm ground
with his toe-tips," and that then, "like that son of earth,

Antæus, he will be strengthened." That is, what we have
seen to be true in the political and scientific world, is
equally true in the realm of Art: the close relation with
Nature, and the devoted service to the trend of life, is a
necessity for a really creative result in this field also.

ACT IV

Act IV deals again with the destructive action of self-
seeking wars.   As the act opens, we see Faust borne
hitherward in a cloud-wrapped car: he finds himself on
that rugged height of Science where he can overlook the
course he has pursued, as Mephistopheles and Faust of
the First Part overlooked the Walpurgis orgy from a
middle height.   We have now to note well that this
cloud, the influence which has brought him onward, assumes, first, the form of the goddess Juno, like the sun,
a Queen of Heaven; it then appears as Leda, suggestive
of the union of the woman and the creative Zeus, the
Father of gods and men; as Helena, the Beauty, the
child of this union, that image of Hellenic civilization;
and we are called on to observe, finally, that this cloud
which bore Faust onward, at last assumes the human
form of that "earliest love," whose self-surrendering
devotion gave the individual Faust of the First Part his
first real glimpse of the Creative, and drew him forth
from his futile study into accord with the stream of active life, the controlling tendency of all existence: it is
the Power of Attraction everywhere manifest in like
manner as the Creative Power.

This new Faust, the image of the race, now scorns the
illusion of pomp and self-satisfaction here offered him
by the Destructive, and says, —

"The deed is everything, the fame is naught."

The remainder of this fourth act is occupied with the subject of the impelling motives of modern warfare, suggested in the figures of the three ruffians "the Bully," "Havequick," and "Holdfast," the comrades of Mephistopheles, the Destructive. We are shown the clash of feudalism and the modern spirit, and the rapacity of the Church; as illustrations of the want of harmony with the creative tendency, which have retarded the progress of civilization and the development of the race into something higher and better.

ACT V

Goethe said that "the Poet should be not only the teacher, but also prophet of mankind." This fifth act is no longer historical, but prophetic of the results of modern tendencies. It opens with a recollection of how the individual Faust was saved from suicide by hearing the songs of faith, and the music of the chapel bell, outside the darkened study. We have here a picture of the shipwrecked sailor, who is saved from the waves of death and brought safely to land by hearing the bell of this decaying old chapel; a poor little property, which Faust wants also to possess in order to erect on its site a scientific observatory.

The destructive tendencies of modern commercial undertakings are suggested, as being similar to those of the warfare pictured in the previous act; and in this connection, Mephistopheles and his three mighty comrades, "Bully," "Havequick," and "Holdfast," are again introduced as coming back from a piratical expedition. They misunderstand Faust's desires, burn down this mouldy old chapel and destroy its ministrants; whom

Faust wished only to remove to a modern dwelling on the new-made land which his activity had created. From the smoke wraiths of the burning chapel four gray figures form themselves, who say their names are "Want," "Crime," "Care," and "Necessity." They surround the "splendid palace" in which Faust now lives: the wraith of "Care" enters through the keyhole and blinds him, so that he "no longer sees the stars."

The explanation of this episode is to be found in that First Part, which Goethe told us would always "announce" what was to follow. There we had the furious rush to get to the top, to the "splendidly-lighted Palace of Mammon"; in which wild orgy the individual Faust forgot and was blinded by the glare, so that he no longer saw that guiding star of his life, the love which he had told Gretchen was the controlling Power that she called God.

In the world-life about him, Goethe had foreseen the growth of materialism, and the consequent failure of mankind to have an adequate conception of the controlling Power above us; like the central attraction of the Sun controlling the stars in their courses. He had also watched the excesses of the French Revolution, and the effect of destroying the mouldy old Church, to enthrone on her desecrated altars the profligate "Goddess of Reason," or Robespierre's vague dream of a "Supreme Being," — a purely speculative, metaphysical conception with no relation to the facts of life.

Here Faust, though blinded, still orders his work for the betterment of humanity to proceed; but history repeats itself, and the "Lemeurs," the spirits of the dead who he imagines are digging his great canal for him, are seen to be really digging his grave. On the brink of that grave he feels, as the result of his services for humanity, that moment of happiness which Mephistopheles had falsely promised the individual Faust of the First Part was to be the result of the selfish pursuit of pleasure.

We note that Faust at last realizes that long-sought and long-desired moment of real happiness; not in the pursuit of pleasure, where the great Deluder had promised him he should find it, but in putting his own life and action into accord with the universal progression of the whole of existence, in being of service to the whole of life.

There is a striking analogy between this weary World-Faust, on the verge of dissolution, and the individual of the First Part, whose story, Goethe told us, would "mirror" the life of the race. That individual had lost all faith in any Controlling Power and was

"Neither afraid of Hell nor th' Devil";

and, as a result, he found himself on the verge of suicide. This World-Faust has not only lost all faith in both God and the Devil, but has succeeded in eliminating from his environment most of those beneficial destructive agencies, which remove the "unfit": he has (*N.B.*) also eliminated those difficulties of life which stir the fit to action. This Faust is then on the brink of dissolution; but we note that though he seems to die, yet even his mortal part "begins to stir" with new forms of life; and "his immortal part," the "entelechy," the mentality active after death, is borne upward and onward by the "Blessed Boys" of the new generations coming from above, the "Angels" with the songs of Creative Love on their youthful lips.

The torch of civilization is never quite extinguished with the fall of the races who have set it alight, but half-extinct, it is relighted and flames again for race after race.

We note here that Mephistopheles, that friend of "The Witch," believes in a revengeful, totally destructive Hell, or at least thinks it

> "does quite well to frighten sinners, yet, however,
> They hold it all for lie, deceit, and dreams."
>
> *Faust*, ii, lines 11,654–57.

He and his attendant Devils have therefore "dragged" this theatrical device of "The Jaws of Hell" upon the stage; wherein we have Goethe's conception of this conventional idea, as being opposed to all that we can observe of the Creative in Nature, as a Power of Love, that uses the destructive elements of life only as a necessary benefit, serviceable to the progression of the whole: death itself being not an absolute destruction, but rather a re-creation into other forms of life more "fit" for the general progressive movement.

> "'T was but appearance, for again it stirred."
>
> *Faust*, ii, line 11,635.

These "Blessed Boys," nearly related to this heavenly Love, sing, as they approach to free the soul of Faust from the Devils who hold the Jaws of Hell, that

> "All Nature's phases
> Are friendly traces,
> Acts of the hovering,
> Lingering flight."
>
> *Faust*, ii, lines 11,681–84.

The flames with which they drive off the Devils are "loving flames," the "roses of love," that "friendly element," which the ignorant boors in "Auerbach's Cel-

lar" mistook for a burning Hell. In the last scene of all,
"The Holy Anchorites," images of certain ecstatic
Fathers of the Church itself, repeat this idea of the beneficial effects of the destructive miseries of life as manifestations of the "Eternal Love." They describe the destructive lightnings, "clearing the air of poisonous
vapours," as the "Messengers of Love"; a statement
which repeats the observation of the Archangel in the
Prologue, who assured us that the destructive lightnings
were the "messengers" clearing the pathway of the
Lord, "the calm progression of His Day."

Herein we see the relation of the so-called "love episode" of Part First to the whole aim of the drama, as the
manifestation of the Creative Control as a Power of
Love; and the reason of Mephistopheles' (the Destructive's) first appearance as being one of "The
Lord's" train of servants.

To visualize his idea of the Creative, as like the re-
producing and sustaining love of the Mother, Goethe
here uses the Church's figure of the "Mater Gloriosa
soaring in heaven"; and the drama closes with exalted
hymns to Creative Love, as the Controlling Power of
life. The possibility of final union with this Power, however Man may have strayed from that "one right way,"
is visualized by the figures of the three great saints,
those repentants, the "Magna Peccatrix," the "Mulier
Samaritana," and "Maria Ægyptiaca," whom the
Church itself represents as selected for special honour,
here shown as praying to the "Glorious Mother" to for-
give the single sin of Gretchen; that destruction of the
new-born life which creative love had given her to
cherish and sustain.

The figure of Gretchen; that "earliest love," is again

introduced as an image of the feminine influence, which
has and will ever lead the hero (Man) upward and onward; a feminine influence to which Goethe, speaking
through the mouth of "Dr. Marianus," bears eloquent
tribute, as having been exercised by Woman as "Virgin,
Mother, Queen, and Goddess."

The drama ends with a "Chorus Mysticus," which
sets forth that all the transitory past (*Vergaengliche*),
which we have seen represented, "is only a symbol" of
that "unattainable" Power manifest in the events here
depicted: —

> "Das Unzulangliche
> Hier wird 's Ereigniss."

The whole meaning of the drama is then summed up
in the statement that this Indescribable Power has here
been shown in the action, as such an eternal feminine
influence, a Power of Attraction ever drawing Man upward and onward to higher development.

> "Das Unbeschreibliche
> Hier ist's gethan;
>   Das Ewig-weibliche
> Zieht uns hinan."

If we reflect that the drama opened with an allusion
to that "highest manifestation of the Creative" as the
Power of Attraction, visible in the feminine power of
attraction of *Die Sonne* (the feminine Sun) holding her
"brother-spheres" on their preordained course; and
that, throughout the drama, we have been shown a like
feminine influence as always bringing man back into the
"one right way" of accord with the Creative, — the
meaning of the whole will be clear to us, as an exposition
of what we can observe thereof in the action of life itself,

as a manifestation of the Power which creates, sustains, and evolves life into "something higher and better."

We shall then understand the Poet's whole intention, and what he meant by saying that "*Faust* opens like a piece of music, with a theme which is carried throughout the whole and repeated at the end."

This outline of the relations of the drama is intended as a "guide-post" to the general direction, such as the "Scholar" asked for "to let one feel one's way about": [1] but, as Goethe remarked: "The poem will explain itself, if we regard it as a whole, and do not undertake to explain the parts separately, and *not* in their relation to each other."

[1] *Faust*, I, line 2008.

CONCLUSION

"To recognize God, where and how he reveals Himself, that is the true blessedness on earth."
(*Maxims and Reflections*, GOETHE.)

THAT, as we have seen, is the real *motif* of Goethe's *Faust;* to call our attention to all the varied sequences of human activity, as ever the same in all phases of life; whereby we may gain for ourselves a conception of the existence and action of that Control which governs the apparently causeless results of action, and thus form for ourselves an incorruptible basis for our religious faith and for the precepts of morality.

"The Moral is an eternal attempt," says Goethe, "to pacify our personal demands and adapt them to the laws of an invisible Realm. Towards the end of the eighteenth century morality had become slack and slavish, as men would subject it to the wavering calculations of a mere theory of the *right to the pursuit of happiness*. Kant first grasped and comprehended the subject in its supernatural significance in his theory of the categorical Imperative; and, though he may have overstrained this idea in his expression thereof, yet he rendered an immortal service in bringing us out of that weakness into which we had sunken."[1]

"If one observes the impulses and actions of mankind for thousands of years, one may recognize some universal formulas that ever, from all time, have exercised a magic power over whole nations as well as over single

[1] *With Riemer*, February 13, 1814, *Bode*, p. 15.

individuals; and these formulas, eternally returning amid thousands of vari-coloured adornments of the same, are the mysterious dower of a Higher Power in life. Each translates these formulas into his own peculiar language, and adapts them in manifold ways to his confined individual conditions; and mixes therewith so much that is impure, ignoble, or the result of self-interest, that they can hardly be longer recognized in their original significance. But this true significance, ever unseen, yet springs forth again; now in this, now in that, people, and the observant investigator constructs for himself, out of these formulas, a kind of alphabet of the World-Spirit."[1]

This is, as Goethe remarks, "that philosophic religion of the sage, who is able to behold and grasp his relation to his fellows and also to the whole of humanity; the relation to all the rest of his earthly environment, both the events which occur as a necessity for the continuance of the movement of life, and those that occur incidentally as the result of chance: such a one lives, in the cosmic sense only, in the Truth." But the religion which Goethe will inculcate in his *Faust* is that "highest unity" of all religions, the religion of awe and reverence for the Higher Power above us, the philosophic religion, which observes the relations of all things, and that "third religion," which he sees most clearly revealed, in his view of the Christian religion, as a "recognition of the Divine also in humility and poverty, scorn and con-

---

[1] *With v. Mueller*, April 29, 1818, *Bode*, p. 16. Dr. Wilhelm Bode has rendered a great service to the student by collating all Goethe's scattered remarks on the subject of Religion in a little pamphlet entitled *Meine Religion, Mein Politischer Glaube*, and the reader who wishes further information on that point is referred thereto.

tempt, shame and misery, suffering and death, yea, even in sin and crime; a recognition and reverence for all these as being not hindrances, but rather as furtherances to what is Holy;"[1] viz.: to that dedication, that universal consecration of all life into something higher and better, to which "The Poet" in the first Prologue said it was his mission to call mankind.

This is that "chief intention" of his *Faust* which, as we have seen, the author has elsewhere pointed out. Into this poem the Poet has poured all his experience of life, his thought, his feelings, his aspirations; and filled it with scintillating flashes of sarcastic wit, and unplumbed deeps of profoundest philosophic wisdom, and — as the "Boy Charioteer," the image of the Poet, suggests — all these are bound together, like the glittering facets of a jewelled necklace, by this central thought of all manifestations of life, as equally a revelation of that Ultimate Cause and Control of Life, to which all being owes its allegiance and existence.

This thought is the *golden key* of life, which will lead us throughout its labyrinthine, mysterious corridors; as Faust was led on to those mysterious goddesses, "The Mothers"; that Mother-Element, the creative force which has produced and ever produces, sustains, and evolves, all things that are.

If, like Faust, we firmly hold this "Key" in hand and with it free ourselves from those "trains of cloud" that trouble our mental vision, we

> "Soon shall note what one in this possesses."
>
> *Faust*, II, line 6262.

[1] See *Wilhelm Meister's Travels*, Book II, Chap. I, pp. 155–57. *Wanderjähre*, pp. 139–141.

If we boldly stir therewith the haply smouldering "tripod" of our own religious faith, we too shall find the hallowed vessel "beams and flashes"; till those incense mists of our involved formulas change indeed into real Gods; whose Olympian Control we recognize and revere as present everywhere in all phases of action, both creative and destructive.

It may be further shown how each smallest incident of the drama is related to this "chief intention," and, in Part I, to the Poet's own experience of life: but this enlightening detail must now be reserved for Notes to the text, which the writer proposes to publish later in connection with an exact translation, that strives also to preserve the rhythmic suggestiveness of the original.

THE END